AF488187

PRAISE FOR MICHAEL LEVIN'S WORK

"Michael understands the need for books to have an appeal for the television and movie market, as well as aspiring writers learning from the great writers of the past. Michael is an intellectual without sounding complicated."
—GARY ALBRECHT

"Writing a book with Michael Levin has been the single biggest accomplishment of my professional career and has elevated me to an elite status in my industry - I couldn't have reached so quickly without Michael's help."
—TATE GROOME, CEO, COLTON GROOME AND COMPANY

"Michael brings years of proven experience, accomplishment, empathy and a deep listening to uncover the stories people don't even know they want to tell."
—DAVID DOWD,
FOUNDER OF CAREER COACHING WITH DAVID DOWD

"Hiring Michael Levin to help me get a book out was the smartest thing I've ever done for marketing my business."
—STEVE MORTON, FINANCIAL ADVISOR

"Michael is a genius with words and was able to put my thoughts on a page eloquently. He is also a real mensch and a great pleasure to work with."
—NEALY FISCHER

"Michael Levin turns 'blah-blah-blah' into 'ah ha!' like no one else on the planet."
—GARY KADI

"Michael and his staff helped me to take some actual events in my life and turn them into a non-fiction novel. They were instrumental in the final design, structure, editing and publishing of my book. I'm so grateful for their professional experience and support!"
—**TIMOTHY PATTEN**

"My father, Victor Carter, was a leading industrialist and philanthropist in Los Angeles for decades. Michael Levin worked with me to capture his story from his upbringing in Russia to his conquering of not one but three industries, including the film industry. Michael was a diligent partner, a thorough interviewer, and an outstanding writer, and I'm very proud of the book that we created together. My father was a true Jewish leader in every sense of the term, and I would recommend Michael to any leader seeking to tell his or her story."
—**FANYA CARTER, AUTHOR,** *ALL THE BEST*

"Thank you for helping make this book possible."
—**ABE ZUCKERMAN, HOLOCAUST SURVIVOR AND AUTHOR,**
A VOICE IN THE CHORUS

"Michael was the ghostwriter for my first book *And You Thought Accountants Were Boring – My Life Inside Arthur Andersen.* From my very first meeting until the book was finally published, Michael was a delight to deal with. He made writing and publishing my first book a fun and beneficial experience. His help made a world of difference."
—**LARRY KATZEN**

"Michael naturally inspires others to realize their true potential. He is a strong witness as a businessman, husband, and father, he is humble and empathetic in the service of others. Michael's zeal with his professional craft as a literary writer will always be a value treasure."
—**GARY MILLER**

"I have had the great fortune to work with Michael on a couple of projects. I will say this, the process was simple and the outcome was remarkable. I entered the process with a general idea of what I wanted to talk on and Michael let me speak. He asked questions. And he was easily able to narrow in on what would make a quality story and book. Michael was quick to provide drafts and always available to discuss the project. Michael has become a friend in the process. And through the time, he has taught what it means to be a great writer."
—MATT REINER, CFA, CFP

"I have worked with Michael on three books, two fiction and a self-help book for attorneys. He has an immensely valuable skill set. His guidance, at the macro and detailed level, greatly improved my books. He is a skilled advisor at each step of a book's path, from concept to review to marketing. With his direction, my novel became an Amazon bestseller and my book for attorneys was employed at a major law school. Five stars, he's the best!"
— WAYNE AVRASHOW, ESQ.

"Michael is the reason why I was able to publish a book. And the finished product is much better than I could have achieved by myself. Michael offers an invaluable service delivered through a true partnership. Simply stated: One of the best decisions I have made in my career."
—MATT SPIELMAN, BUSINESS COACH AND AUTHOR, *INFLECTION POINTS*

"I'm grateful to Michael Levin, who has guided me every step of the way. Michael is a talented author, columnist, and public speaker. Yasher Koach, congratulations on a good job!"
—STEVEN W. KATZ, AUTHOR, *WHO KNEW!*

"When I first heard about Michael Levin, I couldn't quite believe all of the amazing things people we're saying. I didn't know where to begin. How does one write and publish a book that they're proud of? How do I maintain my humor and self-deprecation and still come off as an expert? Michael not only helped me write a winning book proposal, he also found me an agent who helped me negotiate my book deal. The result? *Heart and Sell* hit the Amazon bestseller list. Harvard chose it as the official text book for their Strategic Selling course, and I was able to quintuple my speaking fees! (You read that right). Michael isn't simply a ghost writer and editor, he's a strategist, a humorist, and now, a friend. If you want real direction and expertise, hire him now !!!!!!!!$$$$$$$$$"
—SHARI LEVITIN, AUTHOR, *HEART AND SELL*

"I wrote a book for business students about how I built and sold two successful businesses, so that students could see how I kept my emotional stability through crises and the thinking and effort that goes into such endeavors. Michael guided me to make the book more compelling, better organized, and deeply exciting for readers. Any CEO—or any person—considering becoming an author would benefit from using Michael's services."
—RICHARD JAFFE *TURNING CRISIS INTO SUCCESS: A SERIAL ENTREPRENEUR'S LESSONS ON OVERCOMING CHALLENGE WHILE KEEPING YOUR SH*T TOGETHER*

"Work-life balance implies a zero sum game, compromising on one's professional pursuits, and the rewards they provide, in exchange for being present for oneself, one's family, and one's community. Michael Levin models and explains the win-win alternative by which one grows and contributes on all dimensions synergistically and simultaneously."
—STEVE SPEAR, PROFESSOR, MIT SLOAN SCHOOL OF BUSINESS

"Michael Levin has seriously and judiciously taken the important topic of making money without wasting time. His book prepares you to work smarter instead of harder. Worthwhile reading."
—DR. ALAN KADISH, PRESIDENT, TOURO UNIVERSITY

THE MEANING
OF YOUR LIFE

THE MEANING OF YOUR LIFE

Writing a Book About What Matters Most To You

MICHAEL LEVIN

New York Times Bestselling Author
"The Michael Jordan of Ghostwriting"

Bergen County, New Jersey

The Meaning of Your Life
Writing a Book About What Matters Most To You

Published by The Meaning Company by Michael Levin
Bergen County, New Jersey

www.michaellevinwrites.com

Copyright © 2024, Michael Levin

All rights reserved. No portion of this book may be reproduced in any form without permission from the publisher, except as permitted by U.S. copyright law. For permissions contact: michaellevinwrites@gmail.com

Jacket and book design by Patricia Bacall Garver - www.bacallcreative.com

ISBNs: 979-8-9907199-0-3 Hardcover
979-8-9907199-1-0 Ebook

Printed in United States on acid free paper.

"The best way to make history is to write it."
— Winston Churchill

"What you take with you is what you leave behind."
—Chi Chi Rodriguez

CONTENTS

PART I

THE MEANING MAN TELLS ALL

AN INVITATION –
WHAT MATTERS MOST TO YOU?

It's not a new question.

In *The Canterbury Tales*, written more than 600 years ago, Chaucer asks, "What is life? What does man ask to have?"

An even older quote from a prayer that goes back more than 2,000 years puts it this way: "What are we? What is our life? What is our lovingkindness? What is our righteousness? What saves us? What is our strength? What is our power?"

Human beings have been meaning-seekers and makers since the dawn of time. We have sought to understand our place in the cosmos, our purpose, responsibilities, and destiny ever since our ancestors first gathered around the fire to tell stories. Humans find meaning in a wide variety of domains, including from love to war, service to self-centeredness, and competition to cooperation. While we are busy marrying, raising children, and launching our careers, we don't always have time or focus to devote to the eternal question of why we are here, but as our lives unfold, as we become a little older, more successful, and less caught up in the day-to-day, those questions, which never really went away, can now rise to the fore.

Who are we? What is our life? What is our lovingkindness? What is our strength?

It has been my extraordinary privilege, over the past 35 years, to help people grapple with, and perhaps even solve for themselves, these eternal, essential questions. I am not a theologian or a therapist (although a couple of my clients have written checks to "Dr. Levin!"). I have no special training in the business of helping people find meaning in their lives. I am commonly called a ghostwriter, but that term really doesn't encompass how I serve.

To put it simply, I help people, some extraordinarily successful, some still starting out on life's journey, and some in the middle, answer these vital questions by helping them identify and share with the world what matters most to them, what gives their lives meaning, purpose, and drive. They talk, I type, and the result is a book.

My clients have won the Super Bowl, the NBA Finals, and the World Series. They can be found in the Baseball Hall of Fame and the Forbes List. They are Fortune 10 CEOs, the most respected physicians, dentists, therapists, religious leaders, and authorities in the body, mind, and spirit. They are at the top of their fields in financial services, hedge funds, insurance, accounting, law, politics, technology, consulting, publicity, real estate, philanthropy, entrepreneurship, and coaching in the world of sports. They have rung the bell at the New York Stock Exchange, and they have rung the bell of peace at the World War II shrine in Hiroshima.

Some stories are painful and hard-hitting from individuals who had their lives stripped from them, whether through the loss of a loved one, by enduring sex trafficking, or by surviving the Jewish or Cambodian Holocausts. They came out the other side with a message of hope. They are white, Black, Asian, men, women, young, old, gay, straight, rich, poor ... they run the gamut of human experience. They hail from or have settled in the United States, Canada, Mexico, Latin America, South America, Europe, Australia, and the Far East.

And each of them reached a moment when they realized that whatever financial or professional success they had achieved -and in most cases, we are talking about people at the highest levels of society by any measure -they still needed to do something more with their lives.

They needed to capture, describe, and share what had created meaning in their lives for themselves, their families, their industries, and the world.

They wanted to write a book about the meaning of their lives and what mattered most to them. They did not want to die with their music still in them, in the words of Oliver Wendell Holmes.

They needed to write a book.

Books aren't easy. The ratio of people who would like to be authors to those who have authored a book is probably staggering. It is my job to help people make their books happen. We start off by determining a few key things, as follows:

1. Who is the audience they are trying to influence?
2. What matters most to them?
3. What message would they share with the world if they could get the whole world to sit still and listen?
4. How do we structure that message and all its components into a clear and accessible flow of information from them to the reader?
5. In hours-long conversations, what can they tell me that will allow me to draft a chapter that will be one more link in the information chain between them and the reader?
6. What title and subtitle will capture the readers' attention and explain exactly what benefit they will get from reading the book?
7. How should we publish, distribute, and, if appropriate, market the book to have maximum impact for the audience it is designed to serve?
8. How can we ensure there is value on every page so the reader comes away a different, and perhaps better, person for having read the book?
9. How do we make sure the book is in the client's voice, not in my voice so that no one even suspects the author of the book had help from someone like me?

10. How can we ensure the book captures, as thoroughly, accurately, and beautifully as possible, the author's message so their sense of what gives life meaning shines through and inspires readers to find greater meaning in their lives?

A book isn't just a collection of words on a page; it's also a huge part of your legacy. It's a means of conveying meaning from one person to a million people, from one person today to an audience that can include countless individuals not yet born. Or perhaps it is something less grandiose. It might simply be a way of capturing an individual's story so their grandchildren and great-grandchildren will know who they come from, what they stand for … and perhaps … where the money came from!

What makes your life most meaningful? Is it your family? Your career? Something you invented? Your prowess on the athletic field or in the boardroom? Your creativity? Your love of life? The art you collect? The music you perform? The money, the time, and the wisdom you share with charitable or religious organizations?

As we worked on their books, my clients discovered levels of meaning in their lives they might not have otherwise recognized. The process of doing a book was not simply a recollection and recitation of achievements, personal and professional. Instead, the process itself brought more meaning to their lives by demonstrating to them, and to those around them, in their personal and professional spheres, just how full of meaning their lives truly were.

That is why I encourage you to do your book, whether you write it as a memoir, a business book, a fable, a novel, or what have you. I took one of my favorite life lessons as a frontispiece or quote at the beginning of the book, from the great golfer, the accomplished and affable Chi-Chi Rodriguez, who frequently said, "What you take with you is what you leave behind." Sometimes people describe having a business book as the ultimate leave behind when meeting new prospects. And that's true. The competition has white papers, a folder, or some marketing trinket. Your book is, indeed, the ultimate leave behind, but in a broader sense, the meaning your life creates is the ultimate leave behind for yourself and all those around you. Truly, what we take with us is what we leave behind.

This is a book about the varieties of meaning I have helped transform into books for a wide range of individuals. If you are reading this, perhaps you are considering creating a book that will be a vital part of your legacy, capturing for all time what matters most to you, what is most meaningful to you, and what you most desire to share with the world. Later, I will explain more about the process of how these books came into being, and how yours can, too.

But for now, in thinking about my past clients, more than 1,000 over 35 years, I have found that the most impactful stories resonate deeply with at least one of our basic human needs. As explained by Tony Robbins, we have six essential needs that must be fulfilled if we are to live our best, most enriching lives. These needs are as follows:

- Certainty, the "assurance that you can avoid pain and gain pleasure."
- Uncertainty/ variety, "the need for the unknown, change, new stimuli."
- Significance, "feeling unique, important, special, or needed."
- Connection/ love, "a strong feeling of closeness or union with someone or something."
- Growth, "an expansion of capacity, capability or understanding."
- Contribution, "a sense of service and focus on helping, giving to and supporting others."

Throughout my career, I have been fortunate to help convey the stories of incredible individuals who have shaped their lives around fulfilling these needs, both for themselves and others, and it is my hope that as you read about them, you can decide which of these needs is most meaningful to you.

CHAPTER 1
WHY MEANING MATTERS

In Viktor Frankl's classic work *Man's Search for Meaning*, he says that his fellow prisoners in the Auschwitz death camp were more likely to survive not because they were young and strong but because they had something to live for, something that gave meaning to their lives. Someone they loved and hoped to see again. Compelling work. Religious faith. At Auschwitz, meaning was often the difference between death and life.

And the same rule applies in our world. Meaning changes everything. I was always a huge Zig Ziglar fan. Zig, as he called himself, was a premier motivator, sales trainer, and inspiring individual of his time. As I recount elsewhere in these pages, it was my incredible privilege to edit his last book. Zig loved to tell the story of an individual who passed three workers digging a ditch. He asked each of them what they were doing.

"I'm digging a ditch," the first one said with annoyance, as if the answer wasn't obvious.

"I'm making $17 an hour," said the second.

"I'm building a cathedral," said the third.

The meaning we ascribe to our efforts, situations, and lives dictates the extent to which we find satisfaction and happiness, even in the simplest or most menial tasks.

Or, as Gandhi put it, "What you do is insignificant, but it is essential that you do it."

Sadly, we live in times of great alienation, anxiety, and depression. We have at our fingertips the most magnificent communication devices the world has ever known, yet we feel increasingly isolated. Sometimes, I remind people that there is an app on the phone called "the phone." It actually allows you to hear the voice of another human being in real-time. Instead, we live in a world of silence, where what little contact we have with our fellows is often thin-sliced into a few words of a text or even an emoji meant to capture and convey emotion. How sad.

The great writer Ezra Pound said, "Only connect." Connection leads to purpose, satisfaction, a common cause, and, ultimately, meaning. So, this is a book about people who connected deeply with others, with their world, and with their dreams. In *The Road Less Traveled*, M. Scott Peck talks about the concept of cathexis. It is a profoundly satisfying state in which the separation between you and the object or person with which you are cathexing or connecting on an extremely deep level literally disappears. Peck gives the example of an individual working in her rose garden, when time stands still because she is so absorbed in the work of cutting and pruning.

What do you cathexit with? Where do you achieve that sense of flow state, time standing still, perhaps doing something at work that you would do even if you weren't paid to do it?

There is a concept of two worlds in my faith—this world, the world of work, and the next world, the world to come, an entirely spiritual place known as Olam Ha-Ba. That is the traditional Jewish concept of heaven. The sages teach that we earn our place in Olam Ha-Ba with every good deed we do, while some people earn their Olam Ha-Ba, their place in the next world, in a single moment of action, of grace, of forgiveness, of return. In the pages that follow, you will read stories about people whose entire lives were dedicated to the pursuit of meaning through their work, study, play, connections with others, or love. And then, you will read about others who achieved their Olam Ha-Ba, their immortality, their ticket to the next world, in a single moment when they transcended their limitations and became something bigger, better, and more meaningful than they might ever have imagined.

I'm sharing these stories with you not to make you jealous, but to inspire you to ask, "Where do I find meaning in my life?" It is said that we live our lives forward, but only understand them backwards. This is the moment to look back, despite what Negro League star Satchel Paige used to say: "Don't look back. Something might be gaining on you!"

But seriously. Look back. Where have you found meaning in your life? What will you be remembered for? Our lives can be meaningful even though we aren't perfect. One of the most important takeaways I will share with you later in the book—here's a quick preview—is that your entire life story doesn't have to go into your book. You can draw a curtain around the events that you wish you could have back, or you wish had never happened in the first place. I will describe my Mom's story toward the end of the book. The part that we wanted to preserve for future generations was her early years, not the disappointment of a divorce or the struggles she had with my siblings and me.

I mention all this because sometimes people are concerned that they are not being truthful, or wholly truthful, if they omit certain elements from the recounting of their lives, whether we are talking about their personal lives, business careers, medical practices, or what have you. When you do your own book, you have what they call in Hollywood the "final cut." You get to decide what stays in and what is omitted. It is not about shading the truth; it is about preserving what matters and letting the rest go. Nobody is perfect, and nobody expects a life described in a book to be perfect, either.

Along those lines, I have discovered that when doing memoirs, the first draft is often what I've come to call the "therapy draft." That is where the client gets the whole story out, the good, the bad, and the ugly (sometimes the very ugly!). Then, when the client sees what they said, captured in chapter form in the cold light of day, the response is usually, "Whoa! I can't have that in there!" And out it goes.

A book that seeks to capture meaning is not an opportunity to settle old scores, get back at people, or prove how right you were (at least, not when I'm doing the book). First, there are libel laws. Private figures have a right not to have their reputations besmirched in print. But on top of that, nobody likes a sore winner. If you are doing a book, it is because you have been successful in life. Reminding folks about a situation with a business associate or brother-in-law, even when the other person was clearly at fault, doesn't reflect well on you if you are using your book as a platform for getting even. So, the rule of thumb is that you get to omit the parts of your life experience that you might not want to relive, or you might not want others to know about, and if you are doing things the right way, you don't dig up bones and harm others' reputations. That is just not cricket.

So, to come back to the original subject of this chapter, and of this entire book, really, meaning is what matters. It is not the event—it is not the digging of the ditch—it is the outcome. The building of the cathedral. Your life is a cathedral. You built it, and now, it is time to step back and admire your handiwork. Yes, we stand on the shoulders of giants, and yes, perhaps there was a spiritual dimension to your success that you would like to give credit to the Being that gave you the ability to do what you do, or not. But there comes a time in every person's life when she gets to say, "How did I get here? How did this happen?" Not just because she wants the answers to those questions, but because others—some alive now, some not yet born—will want the answers, too.

What if you don't remember it exactly? Who cares! Memory is a funny thing. It is not a smartphone recording every word that was said, every gesture, every nuance. It is just our best attempt to reconstruct and understand what happened. Nothing wrong with that. It is often an iterative process. We talk, you get the draft back, and that triggers other memories or corrections to the memories we have already captured. That is part of the fun, reawakening experiences buried in our subconscious and happily conducting them to the light of day.

Along those lines, a book that captures of the meaning of your life isn't an obituary! They aren't shoveling dirt on you just yet! I always tell my clients, "Think of it as an interim report, not a final report." In other words, this is what you have learned, this is what you have experienced, this is what you have seen, this is what you have built … up to the current moment. As more happens, we will revise accordingly or do another book down the road! So, you don't have to worry about the fact that you still have more to create, more to offer, more to give.

As I said a moment ago, I'm not presenting the stories in this book to make you jealous. I will never be in the Baseball Hall of Fame, or amass a billion-dollar art collection, or own a Major League Baseball team (like one of my clients who isn't in this book), or lead my family to safety through the forest during the Cambodian holocaust. Instead, me sharing the purpose of the stories behind some of the books I have done is to "wake up the echoes," as they say at Notre Dame, to get you thinking about where you find meaning in your life, and perhaps where others have found it in your life, too. Maybe it will be a business story. Maybe it will be something of a more personal nature. That is the beauty of life. We are all different, we all have a role to play, and we all contribute. So, what matters most to you? That is the real question, as opposed to asking, "Is my life more or less meaningful than the ones in this book?"

When he speaks about the six human needs, Tony Robbins points out that we all possess all six to some degree. It is just that typically two stand out for each of us. For one person, it is connection and growth. For someone else, it is variety and contribution. As you go through the stories, ask yourself which two of the six essential human needs are most meaningful to you. After each set of stories, I will share some guidance on how those books are written, and some questions for you to think about. I hope you enjoy the stories behind the books as much as I enjoyed the process of creating them. So, let's get started.

I hope these stories about others who asked those ancient questions—who are we, what is our life, what makes us righteous, what makes us strong—whether from Chaucer or the prayer book, get you thinking about what matters most to you. First, though, I'll tell you the story of how I got here. And when I say there was no plan, believe me!

CHAPTER 2
MY STORY

Lives have turning points, or "hinges," as some people say. For me, two such turning points happened within weeks, and as a result, I had a sense of purpose and the skills I would need to live that purpose. Although I certainly didn't understand that at the time.

As my sophomore year at Amherst College was ending, I was invited to the Classics Department's annual year-end party. It was the 1970s, so there were no rules. And classicists, at least at Amherst, had a reputation for outdrinking every other department on campus.

I had never tried shots of tequila, lime, and salt before. I don't think I felt the first eight or nine. The tenth or eleventh hit home, though, and by the twelfth or fourteenth—if you can remember how many you had, you didn't have that many—I actually silenced the entire room and swore that since they were the greatest people in the world, I would become a Greek major in my last two years at school.

My drunken word became my sober bond. I did four years of Greek over the next two years and completed a major in ancient Greek alongside my previously planned major in English literature.

Let me tell you what it means to study ancient Greek. You are in small classes ranging from two to nine people. You are responsible for translating 40 lines of text from, say, Plato, Sophocles, Aristophanes, or Herodotus three times a week. You must then come to class prepared to be called on to explain any one of those 40 lines. Greek is complicated. A word could be a noun, a verb, singular, plural, any of four cases, and so on. Because Greek is an "inflected" language, words don't have to go in the correct order. Inflected means that the endings of the words tell you whether they are nouns, verbs, adjectives, adverbs, or what have you, and whether they are singular, plural, male, female, and so on.

A line like "Shall I compare thee to a summer's day?" in Greek could appear as "compare day thee I shall summer's"—and since they didn't have punctuation, good luck figuring out that it's a question. So, to study Greek, you need a magnifying glass and a Sherlock Holmes cap because you are not just a reader, you are also a detective. You are putting together puzzles within puzzles. I had a study partner, and she and I would work for about four hours together in the student lounge, trying to crack the code on each of those 40 lines, three times a week. Then we would each go back to our own dorm rooms and spend another three hours polishing what we had done. The idea of letting down our professor by not having precise knowledge of every single syllable was unthinkable. So that's how I spent my last two years of college, and the summer between junior and senior year— staring intently at 120 lines of Greek every week.

What did I learn? First, to ask, in any given situation, how important will this be in 2,500 years? That is the kind of perspective you get when you are studying literature that old.

Second, the ability to sit still and stare at words. Diamond cutters work with diamonds. Jewelers work with precious metals. Writers work with words, our jewels, our precious metals. I learned to sit there and stare at those words and understand with the utmost level of clarity and precision exactly what had been written 25 centuries earlier.

When my mom came up to visit, we had coffee with my Greek advisor, who asked her, "How does it feel to have a son who is studying dead languages?" The implication was that there was nothing less marketable than what I was doing. It transpires that nothing could have been further from the truth. Sitting there and staring at Greek for all those endless hours turns out to have been the perfect preparation for what I do now. I still stare at words. I still aim for the utmost level of clarity and precision. Of course, these days, the words are all in English, which makes life considerably easier.

A month after my Greek bacchanal, I clerked for a small civil rights law firm in Midtown Manhattan. One morning, they sent me to deliver some papers to the New York State Office Building on 125th Street in Harlem. I had never been to Harlem before, and I must admit the subway ride to 125th Street was an uneasy experience for me, a 20-year-old from the suburbs. I found the building and the correct office where I was supposed to deliver the papers.

The woman behind the counter, who was Black and probably in her 50s, studied me, which felt odd. She suddenly exclaimed, "Your father is Emil Levin!"

I could not have been more shocked.

"Emil Levin is my grandfather!" I replied, astonished that she could have seen any resemblance between my grandfather, who, in my mind, was an old man, and me, a kid of 20.

My grandfather had been in politics and community service for almost half a century. He was involved in philanthropy, race relations, the State of Israel, mental health organizations, the Y … you name it. He had even run for Congress twice, unsuccessfully. Some of my earliest memories include visiting his campaign headquarters and riding on his sound truck in the 1964

Emil Levin, for the people. Did I really look like him?

election when I was six years old. I actually gave him some really brilliant campaign advice.

"If the voting is tied when the polls close," I told him, with all the confidence a six-year-old can muster, "that's when you go up and vote. That way, you will win."

The advice didn't help, but my grandfather was subsequently appointed to the New York State Human Rights Appeals Board, which heard cases relating to racial discrimination in housing and employment. His office was on the 82nd floor of a building you may have heard of, the World Trade Center.

But now, here I was, face to face with a woman who not only knew my grandfather but could see his features in mine.

"Your grandfather is a good man," she told me. "Your grandfather is *for the people*."

The experience was stunning and far more than I had bargained for when I took the subway from Midtown to Harlem. I now had a standard by which to live my life. Like my grandfather, I, too, would be "for the people."

But how?

• • •

I fell in love with books when my father read me *Ask Mr. Bear*, a children's book, before bedtime. The idea that someone would take your words, your thoughts, and then bind them into a book and send them out into the world … even as a little kid, I found the concept mind-blowing!

Fast forward to third grade. The school librarian, Miss Wood, as she was known (it was the 1960s, people) was incredibly frightening and stern if you lost a library book. I lost plenty, so I should know! One day, she showed our class a film strip about how books were created. One image depicted an author reviewing his galleys, his manuscript laid out in page form, the last step before publishing.

That's me, I told myself, and that has been me throughout my entire adult life.

Books are magic. They entertain, they educate, they tell stories, they bring clarity, and they help make people better at life. Writing is all I've ever wanted to do, and I'm incredibly blessed that this is how I make my livelihood, how I serve. And yes, I knew it from that day in third grade. Thank you, Miss Wood!

The first time I ever published anything was in 1972, when I was 14 and fascinated by politics. I wrote a short letter to Time Magazine after the appointment of Henry Kissinger to the position of Secretary of State. "Sir," my letter began, "Mr. Kissinger lends a touch of class to a very unclassy Administration."

Well, *Time* considered my opinion worthy of sharing with the world, and my mind was blown all over again. I followed up with letters to Newsweek and The New York Times. You see your name and words in print in a national publication, while still a teenager, and you start thinking, maybe I can do this.

When I was 16, I attended a summer program in London where we got to meet playwrights and directors. Tom Stoppard,

fresh from his success with a play called *Travesties*, came to our class and had lunch with us. Nice young guy. Wonder whatever became of him. The most remarkable moment of that summer, however, was visiting a bookstore that no longer exists, Foyle's Annex, where they only sold

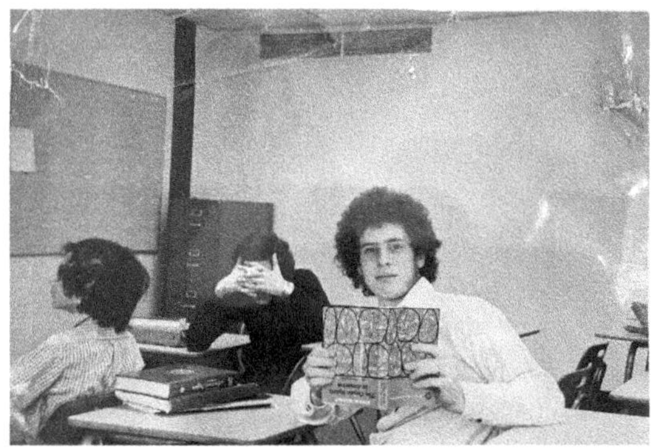

Portrait of the artist as a young wingnut.
Roslyn High School, 1974

Penguin paperbacks. On the walls were caricatures of the great authors they published, including James Joyce, William Faulkner, and George Orwell, and I was struck by what seems like the most obvious thing in the world, but to me, it came as a thunderclap. *These authors were actual human beings.* They weren't gods on Mt. Olympus tossing down manuscripts like thunderbolts. They were people. I was people. Maybe I could be one of them. Maybe …

I went to Amherst College, where I majored in English and Ancient Greek, and also studied French, Latin, and Middle English. I fell in love with words and sentences. That is what nerds do, we fall in love with words and sentences. Girls and drinking and all that, but primarily words and sentences. In the evenings, I would sometimes wander the stacks of the college library, said to contain half a million volumes. I would stare at all those books and ask myself, could I conceivably be a worse writer than all half million of those authors? Even if I was at the bottom of the list, surely, I was in there somewhere. Wasn't I?

I wrote for the student newspaper, and one night, while we were putting the paper to bed, our offices were taken over by one of the student groups. It was the 70s; that's what one did. There were about 16 to 18 editors, and we all crammed into the chairman's office, as the senior editor was known, to discuss how we would cover our own takeover in the next day's edition.

I started taking notes for the story. There was never any discussion; it was just sort of assumed by all present that I would write the cover story about the takeover for the next day. When I was done writing the story, it hit me. Those kids at Amherst were really smart. Really good writers. By contrast, I got in off the waiting list by the skin of my teeth, and not because of my grades or SATs. And yet, they all understood that I was the writer to be entrusted with that story. That blew my mind.

While at Amherst, I subscribed to The New York Times. Everybody did back then, or so it seemed. It was probably $5 for the entire school year to have the paper delivered to your dorm room. One morning, during my junior year, I was reading an opinion piece and found myself impressed by the writing and the points the author was making. Who was it? To my surprise, it was a college student, also a junior, at some other school. That got my attention. This kid is my age, and he's published in The New York Times?

The summer after I graduated, I had an idea for an opinion piece. I was a huge Art Buchwald fan and wrote a story in his style. I submitted it—that means I typed it out and mailed it in an envelope with a stamp— to the opinion page editor. A few days later, the phone rang. It was an editor at the Times. They were publishing

the piece. I drove into the city every night for a week to get the early or "bulldog" edition of the Times, to see if my story was there. And then, one night … August 22, 1980 … there it was. Seeing my name and my words … it felt like being hit by lightning all over again. I sent in another opinion piece two years later, and they published that one, too. And then that second piece ended up in a textbook on writing, alongside Plato and Woody Allen.

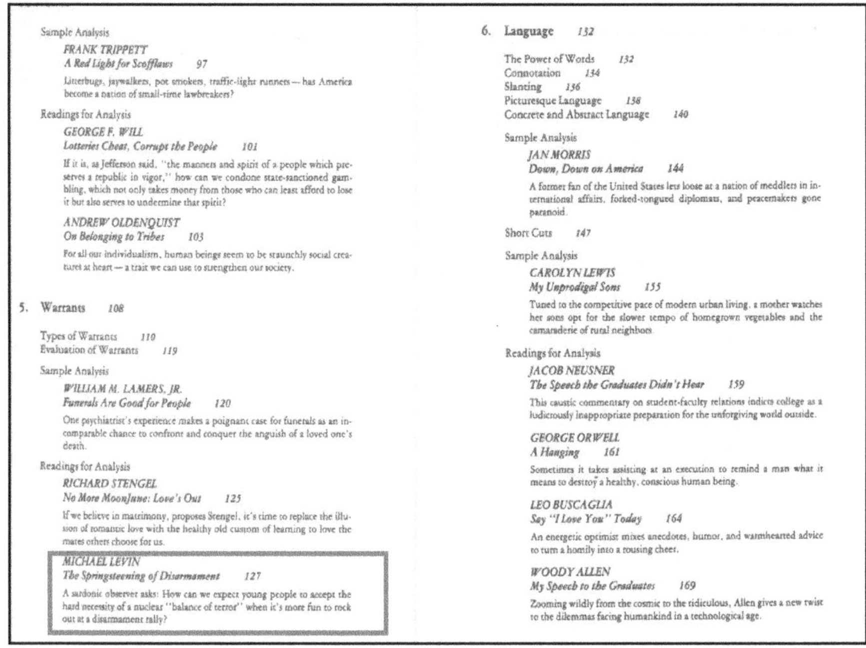

Sample Analysis
  FRANK TRIPPETT
  A Red Light for Scofflaws   97
  Litterbugs, jaywalkers, pot smokers, traffic-light runners — has America become a nation of small-time lawbreakers?

Readings for Analysis
  GEORGE F. WILL
  Lotteries Cheat, Corrupt the People   101
  If it is, as Jefferson said, "the manners and spirit of a people which preserves a republic in vigor," how can we condone state-sanctioned gambling, which not only takes money from those who can least afford to lose it but also serves to undermine that spirit?

  ANDREW OLDENQUIST
  On Belonging to Tribes   103
  For all our individualism, human beings seem to be staunchly social creatures at heart — a trait we can use to strengthen our society.

5. Warrants   108

  Types of Warrants   110
  Evaluation of Warrants   119

  Sample Analysis
  WILLIAM M. LAMERS, JR.
  Funerals Are Good for People   120
  One psychiatrist's experience makes a poignant case for funerals as an incomparable chance to confront and conquer the anguish of a loved one's death.

  Readings for Analysis
  RICHARD STENGEL
  No More MoonJune: Love's Out   125
  If we believe in matrimony, proposes Stengel, it's time to replace the illusion of romantic love with the healthy old custom of learning to love the mates others choose for us.

  MICHAEL LEVIN
  The Springsteening of Disarmament   127
  A sardonic observer asks: How can we expect young people to accept the hard necessity of a nuclear "balance of terror" when it's more fun to rock out at a disarmament rally?

6. Language   132

  The Power of Words   132
  Connotation   134
  Slanting   136
  Picturesque Language   138
  Concrete and Abstract Language   140

  Sample Analysis
  JAN MORRIS
  Down, Down on America   144
  A former fan of the United States lets loose at a nation of meddlers in international affairs, forked-tongued diplomats, and peacemakers gone paranoid.

  Short Cuts   147

  Sample Analysis
  CAROLYN LEWIS
  My Unprodigal Sons   155
  Tuned to the competitive pace of modern urban living, a mother watches her sons opt for the slower tempo of homegrown vegetables and the camaraderie of rural neighbors.

  Readings for Analysis
  JACOB NEUSNER
  The Speech the Graduates Didn't Hear   159
  This caustic commentary on student-faculty relations indicts college as a ludicrously inappropriate preparation for the unforgiving world outside.

  GEORGE ORWELL
  A Hanging   161
  Sometimes it takes assisting at an execution to remind a man what it means to destroy a healthy, conscious human being.

  LEO BUSCAGLIA
  Say "I Love You" Today   164
  An energetic optimist mixes anecdotes, humor, and warmhearted advice to turn a homily into a rousing cheer.

  WOODY ALLEN
  My Speech to the Graduates   169
  Zooming wildly from the cosmic to the ridiculous, Allen gives a new twist to the dilemmas facing humankind in a technological age.

Despite all that, I couldn't figure out how writers made a living, so I went to law school. Three years of law school, and then two stints of five months each at two firms. I was all but fired from the first firm and then fired from the second because they could tell I didn't want to be there. My work product wasn't great, my hours were low (but honest), and they could tell it wouldn't work out with me. I tried to get a job at a third firm. I interviewed well and had a great resume, but once they called the prior firms for references, I was sunk and unemployable.

By then, I had sold two novels to Simon & Schuster and would soon sell a third. While thrilling, the money was low, and after a while, it ran out. I was literally a starving writer. At the same time as my Columbia Law School classmates were making partner at major firms in New York and elsewhere, I was literally on heating assistance because my income was below $13,000 a year. Not a party.

With Howard Cosell, who interviewed me on his nationally syndicated radio show, "Speaking Of Everything," after my first novel, The Socratic Method, *was published*

On January 31, 1994, I had $35,000 worth of credit card debt, $900 a month of minimum payments to make, and no income. I went to a recovery group that specialized in people like me who had problems with money and debt. I met a man who would mentor me for the next 29 years. He showed me how to start a business, which initially consisted of offering writing classes in a rented space; first, the yoga studio I attended and then, a meeting room in a church in Boston's Back Bay. Some of my students asked if I would consult on their projects on an hourly basis, and that led to some of them saying, "Just write it for me." And that's how I literally backed into a career of ghostwriting and private biography.

According to Michael Gerber, who created the E-Myth business books, which have sold millions of copies over the decades, no one has created more successful books than I have. I have been called the "Michael Jordan of private biography." So how do you end up doing all these books with celebrities, sports figures, broadcasters, top athletes, members of the Forbes List, billionaires, doctors, dentists, consultants, financial services professionals, and on and on?

When I tell you there was no plan, trust me, *there was no plan.* Instead, I was fortunate enough to build a ghostwriting practice that has encompassed more than 1,000 books in one shape or another over the past three decades—writing them, planning them, editing them, consulting on them, publishing them, and, in a few cases, agenting them. I still love words and sentences. I'm still a nerd. Capturing and disseminating ideas that make the lives of other people better - whether we are talking business and finance, body, mind, spirit and health, sports and broadcasting, consulting, or what have you - remains as thrilling to me today as it was the first time I put pen to paper.

Incredibly, it has been more than half a century since I sent Time Magazine that two- sentence letter praising Henry Kissinger. Why I sent it, I couldn't have told you then, and I certainly couldn't tell you now, but the thrill of seeing words and ideas in print never grows old. That's how it has been for my clients, and I hope that's how it will be for you, too.

Writing books for other people was never my career choice. In fact, it was a career I had never heard of, but it turns out there is really nothing better that I could have done with the last 35 years. I like to say that I only have two qualifications for clients—they have to be positive people with a positive message. That message might have to do with business and finance, medicine or dentistry, body, mind, spirit, or sports, or what have you.

Think about it like this. Over here, you have an individual with ideas that could transform the lives of countless people, if only they could be captured in book form. That person typically doesn't have the time, the desire, or sometimes the ability to write his or her own book. And over there, you have a specific audience—what Seth Rogan calls a tribe—of people whose lives would be improved if only they had access to this person's thinking.

I get to stand in the gap.

I get to listen to the tribal leader with the ideas to share, while standing in the shoes of the reader, and then I get to express those ideas in the author's voice so that they improve, benefit, uplift the life of the reader.

I have always called my job the greatest graduate school on the planet because I am constantly learning from the people who are the best in their fields. And then I get to turn around and share that knowledge with the audience that needs to hear from those individuals most.

I've done my share of books with celebrities, broadcasters, and sports figures. I really don't need to do another celebrity book. I'm much more interested in private individuals who have a wealth of knowledge that needs to be captured and shared, not as an act of vanity but as an act of service, so that the lives of their fellow men and women might be better.

I am humbled to say that the books I have written, planned, edited, or published have touched the lives of millions and millions of individuals and families.

I never saw that coming when I ghosted my first book.

I never saw it coming, the idea that I might be involved with more than a thousand books.

Alfred Hitchcock used to say that he made movies about ordinary people thrust into extraordinary circumstances. That is what made them so relatable and compelling. In a way, you could say the same thing about my clientele. They are ordinary people in the sense that most of them are not instantly recognizable celebrities, or people with massive social media presences, for whatever that is worth.

Instead, they are people who have lived their lives as best they can, from a professional, community-minded, or spiritual perspective. And they have achieved extraordinary accomplishments. If they had a flock of birds chasing after them, they could be heroes in a Hitchcock film! The serious point is that these individuals have so much to share, and I get to serve as the force multiplier for their wisdom.

My grandfather, who was "for the people," passed away before I started my ghostwriting career, although I was able to give him a copy of my first novel, *The Socratic Method*, which Simon & Schuster published in 1986, the month before he died. I never expected to be a private biographer, which is the term I use to describe what I do, but in my own small way, it is how I am for the people. The 20-year-old standing, shocked, in the New York State Office Building in Harlem back in 1978 would probably be surprised that this is the way he eventually found to be "for the people." I would like to think he would be pleased. I know I am.

CHAPTER 3

A GHOST ON ABC'S SHARK TANK

I was sitting outside in the sunshine at a trendy restaurant on Olympic Boulevard in Los Angeles interviewing the executive producer on Shark Tank, which was in the middle of its second season, for a client's book. He was telling me about one amazing entrepreneur after the next who had been on the show. I have to admit that I felt somewhat "less than" as I listened to his tales of Congressional aides creating barbeque sauce, a woman who invented a self-cleaning litter box for cats, and so on. What did I do for a living? Nothing *that* interesting.

"Let me ask you a question," said the executive producer, a man named Brien Meagher. "Have you ever thought about appearing on our show?"

I looked over at my assistant, who was sitting in and listening, to make sure I had heard him correctly. His question knocked me speechless.

"But there's nothing sexy about my business," I protested, when I could finally find my voice again. "It's just me in a room, typing."

He shook his head.

"I disagree completely," he said. "I think your business is very sexy. I would like you to apply for the show."

Back then, as Season Three began, more than 30,000 entrepreneurs applied to be on Shark Tank. Of those 30,000, only about 110

27

were invited to come to Los Angeles to tape segments with the Sharks. Of those roughly 110 segments, only about 35 made it to air. So, if you were an entrepreneur and you appeared on Shark Tank Season Three, you overcame odds of 1,000 to one.

Unless you were me.

If the executive producer of a show wants you on a show, guess what, kids? You're getting on the show. So I did all the things that were asked of me. I shot a video explaining who I was and what my business was about. I talked to my business friends to determine how much to ask for. I passed each test (no surprise since the wheels were greased). I worked on my opening pitch with the line producer I had been assigned until we had it polished to a high sheen. And then, the fateful day arrived.

"You're going to tape," he said. "Congratulations!"

The entire years' worth of segments with entrepreneurs are taped over on Labor Day weekend. The Sharks know nothing about you prior to your coming on the air. When you see them writing down how much you're asking for and what your business is worth, that's the first time they've ever heard anything about you. So, if you've ever wondered whether the show is real or not, trust me, it's real.

The Sharks are not bound by deals they make because they can perform their due diligence after they've hugged it out with you in the tank. The show is as real as real could be. The night before I taped, they put me up in a hotel in West Los Angeles not far from the Sony lot. I took a van to the studio with my props and with a few other contestants. My line producer had me stand outside the studio and shout out my memorized opening pitch several times at the top of my lungs, to do a final rehearsal, and then to get rid of any butterflies. That was a very strange experience – yelling that I'm a ghostwriter outside a soundstage at Sony Studios. Definitely a one-of-a-kind moment.

And then it was time. I walked down the corridor the same way you see the contestants enter on the show. I felt as if I'd been somehow miniaturized sufficiently so that I could fit inside my television set. I got to the carpet where the entrepreneurs stand, and then I had to stand there for about a minute and a half. It's awkward. You're looking at the Sharks and the Sharks are looking at you, but nothing happens until the camera people say they are ready. So I just stood there and smiled, and they smiled at me, and then I got the go-ahead. I made my pitch.

Truth be told, it just wasn't their kind of business. I'm not a fireman with a new kind of nozzle for fire hoses, or a Breathometer that attaches to your iPhone. I knew that going in, but the opportunity to go on the show was too exciting to pass up. So I stood there, made my presentation confidently, and then the floor was open. They all shouted questions at once, and it reminded me of Moot Court in law school, where judges and lawyers come in and pretend they are an appellate court, peppering you with questions as you try to make your case.

I had done all the homework I could on the Sharks, reading about their interests, reading about the books they had purportedly written, and otherwise getting to know them. They were actually friendly and respectful. I had no idea how brutal the Sharks could be to entrepreneurs who came in with a line of blarney and no track record with sales.

The short of it is that none of them invested, which makes sense because my business was not scalable in the way a Shark Tank business must be. I hadn't come up with a breakthrough idea for women's gym clothing. I was a guy who wrote books. One Shark, Robert Herjavec, paid me a great complement on national television. "You've done what practically no writer has ever done. You figured out how to make a business, and a very successful business, about writing."

For me, that was the most valuable takeaway from the whole experience. Yes, the phone rang a lot after the show aired. Yes, it became a significant part of my marketing, since I was the ghostwriter you saw on Shark Tank, and it gave me the experience and credibility to sell my business. But the complement mattered to me, because until then, I had felt that slight level of shame about the fact that I hadn't "made it" as a novelist, which had always been my dream.

I sold the first three novels I ever wrote to Simon & Schuster and could never come to terms on a fourth, although I sold several other novels a few years later. The real dream was to sit poolside somewhere, tossing off novel after novel, and making crazy sums of money. Since that hadn't happened, the writing classes, and then the coaching and ghostwriting I offered, felt like a fallback or almost an admission of failure. I felt as if I was taking in washing. So to suddenly get the stamp of approval from these wealthy, successful entrepreneurs, and to receive it on national television, changed the way I saw myself. Suddenly, I wasn't a failed novelist; I was a successful entrepreneur. I could take pride in what I had accomplished. That was truly a life-changing moment for me.

CHAPTER 4

HOW BOOKS HAPPEN (AND HOW THEY SOMETIMES DON'T!)

The hardest clients to satisfy are those who have been burned by a prior writer. Not only did they lose trust in the writer they had hired, but they had also lost trust in the whole concept of bringing someone in to work with them on a book.

Writers disappoint their clients in many ways. Some just don't show up. They take the upfront fee and then good luck getting them to respond to an e-mail or text.

Then you have the ones who *do show up* but do a lousy job. The client is stuck. The agreement may allow for refunds in the event of client dissatisfaction, but a lot of the time, writers just simply don't have the money to pay back. It is a precarious, hand-to-mouth existence for writers who are not established or who don't have good financial skills. And if the client wants to sue them, what exactly will they win in court? The writer's socks?

Then you have writers who show up, respond to phone calls and e-mails, and actually turn in a complete draft. The challenge here is that most ghostwriters are somewhat afraid of their clients. After all, the clients are older, richer, and far more accomplished. As a result, the writer questions exactly what they have to offer the client. They

31

let the client drive the entire process, with predictably poor results. A writer must be able to step in and say, "Let's talk about this, and let's talk about that some other time. Right now, we need to focus on this." But if you are afraid of your client, or in awe of her, how exactly are you going to manage that feat? The easiest course is to let the client lead the process, but that is not what they are paying the writer for. When successful people sense the person they are working with is inexperienced or, worse, fearful, their need for control kicks in. And now we are on a steep, slippery slope for a project that is either never completed or not completed well.

In these cases, the writer is sometimes too afraid even to suggest talking through an outline for the book. Instead, the client just starts talking, and the writer feels obliged to somehow keep up with the conversation. The writer, in this all too frequent scenario, will schedule endless meetings with the client, where they talk about pretty much anything that is on the client's mind on any given day. This can go on for 20 or 30 hours, or even longer. At the end of it, the writer now has hundreds of pages of transcripts to wade through. He has the challenging task of trying to find a book in all that material. Six months later, the writer will present a manuscript to the client based on those meandering conversations, but unfortunately, neither the client nor the writer has any recollection of what they were talking about. The resulting manuscript has practically no value at all, even if the writer has managed the feat of writing in the client's voice. It is a total waste of time and money. No wonder people feel burned when they get this kind of result.

So here's a quick primer on what to consider when you are hiring a writer, whether it is me or anyone else. And after that, I will share with you my approach to organizing and writing books.

First, how well does the writer present herself on her website? Does the writer even have a website? Does it look professional, or does it look like something that hasn't been updated since the early 90s? These days, it doesn't take much time, money, or effort to create an attractive website, which is the most obvious form of self-presentation. My late, great Russian lit professor, Stanley Rabinowitz, used to say that you *can* judge a book by its cover. If a book is poorly designed and the cover is unattractive, chances are that the book (or the translation if it is something foreign) isn't any good, either. It is the same thing with writers. You can judge a writer by their website.

On the website, note exactly what services the writer provides. Some writers list the fact that they do blog pieces, speeches, white papers, and books. Seriously? Books are a different animal. If the writer you are considering lists books as only one of the things that she does, be afraid. Be very afraid. Jacks of all trades are typically masters of none. Book writing is simply different from other forms of writing. Don't ask a sprinter to run a marathon. Don't hire a generalist. Get someone who only talks about books, or maybe books and speeches, on her website.

With Erica Jong, a mentor of mine and the author of Fear Of Flying, *which sold 20 million copies*

Next, on the website, are there blurbs from past clients? The writer does not need to have best sellers on her website to be credible (although it never hurts). At a minimum, you want to see quotes from happy clients whose job titles are impressive to you. Yes, ghostwriting is typically confidential, but many clients will be happy to give words of praise to their writers if they have done a great job. If there are no blurbs from past clients, that is a serious red flag.

You also want to see if the writer has worked with people at your level. If you are the CEO of a Fortune 100, do you really want to work with someone who has never done a book for a high-level executive? Do you really want to be the first? It is entirely possible that a writer who has done a fine job for local businesspeople could step up in class and do a great job for you, but wouldn't you rather work with someone who already has experience with people in your world? Something to think about.

Let's say the writer has already passed these tests and they have a solid website with blurbs from enthusiastic clients like you. So, you reach out and have a conversation with the writer. Ask about their process. Make sure they have one! If it is simply, "We talk a lot, and then I write the book, and you get it six months from now," then buyer, beware. Do they have a clear, detailed process for how they get this done? Does the process they describe inspire confidence? If not, there are plenty of other fish in the writing sea.

While you are on the phone, ask the writer if they have past clients with whom you can speak. If not, that is a red flag. Yes, as we have noted, ghostwriting is typically a confidential process, but any accomplished writer will have plenty of past clients who will be happy, even eager, to take your call and sing the writer's praises. If that is not the case, there is probably a reason why.

So, by now, the writer you are considering has checked a lot of boxes. Their website is solid. They focus only on books, or perhaps books and speeches. They have great blurbs, and is willing to let you speak with past clients. He has a process that he detailed on the call with you, and the process is something other than wasting a lot of your precious time and hoping that a book miraculously emerges. Now it is time to talk about fees and agreements.

Here's where the rubber meets the road. Does the writer have an actual standard agreement? Some do, many don't. It is a huge red flag if they don't. This is their business. Any business should have a standard agreement, which may be modified from case to case. Your writer ought to specify, in writing, the project fee, triggers for payments, how many hours of interview time you can expect, how long the book will be (measured in words or pages), refund terms, and so on. If your writer is savvy, the agreement will include a confidentiality clause that protects your privacy and a choice of venue clause that protects his right not to be sued out of state. If you don't see most or all these things on the agreement, you have got to ask yourself whether you are really dealing with someone professional.

I've always offered prospects a "test drive" option of the book plan plus the first two chapters for a small fee, which will be applied to the overall project fee should the client decide to go forward. Test drives are great because they allow you, the client, to see what it is like to work with this particular writer. Do you like the process? Are you happy with the work? A test drive keeps you from having to make a big bet of your time, money, and hope. See if your writer offers one or is open to offering you one. From my perspective, although I don't share this fact with the client, it is an opportunity for me to see what it is like to work with a given individual. My practice is limited to positive people with a positive message, but you can't always tell from a sales call. Sometimes it takes getting into the project before you can see a person's true colors. So the test drive phase allows me to find a respectful way to end an engagement without hard feelings or recourse to attorneys.

Now that you have seen all the different ways that writers can disappoint their clients, I can understand if you are a little squeamish about the whole idea of bringing on a writer. But at least you now know how to reduce the possibility of a bad outcome, because you know the red flags that flap in the breeze alongside writers you should never have hired in the first place. Okay. Time for some sorbet to cleanse the palate. Let's move on to the question of the right way to get a book done. Or at least one right way ... the way that has worked for me for all these years.

On the first call with a prospective client, I have two related questions. First, what is the purpose of the book? What do you hope to accomplish? And second, if we were talking six months after the book came out, what would have to happen for you to decide that the project was a success?

I ask these things because, many times, people simply don't know what to expect when they do a book, or they have expectations that are simply out of line with reality. One of the hardest things in the world today is to sell books to strangers. Give them away? Easy button. Sell them back of the room when you are doing a keynote? Love that! Print them for $3 and sell them for $30. That is a nice day at the office. But when I hear, "I don't expect this book to be a New York Times bestseller," what I really hear them saying is, "I expect my book to be a New York Times bestseller, and if it isn't, it is because you screwed the whole thing up."

That's a bright red flag.

I tell prospective clients I'm an attorney by training, and that in the field of ghostwriting or private biography, *malpractice consists of creating false hope*. Then, I explain to them what is possible and what is unlikely with a book they have in mind. Usually, they are very grateful for the reality check and are happy that someone is telling them the truth instead of blowing smoke and creating hype. So now we can have a serious conversation about the process because the client's expectations about potential outcomes are in line with reality.

What can happen when you do a book? I always say that magic happens, but you can just never predict the direction from which the magic will come. You never know who will see the book. You never know who will reach out to you to be your client, your partner, your investor, or your friend. You have no idea when the news media will come across your book and want to interview you. Books are force multipliers. They get your ideas, your name, and your brand out into the world in ways that white papers, LinkedIn profiles, or social media never can. There is a certain cachet to being an author, a certain sense of dignity, uniqueness, respectability, and thoughtfulness. It is your opportunity to demonstrate preeminence, to remove yourself from the pit of commoditization, to capture your life story and experience for all time. Try getting *that* with an Instagram post.

So how are we going to accomplish this in the most effective way?

I developed my process decades ago when a client referred me to a self-made tech billionaire who wanted a book to capture the culture of his rapidly growing enterprise. I remember actually hitting my knees in prayer in the elevator on the way to his Century City office, asking myself what on earth does a billionaire need someone like me for? And the divine answer came back quickly: "He needs a book, you moron!"

I got off my knees and got to work.

I learned back then that highly successful people are extremely busy, and they typically don't get less busy as time goes on. Highly successful individuals, and I'm sure that you will identify, attract endless numbers of opportunities in their work lives and in their personal lives. When they think about doing a book, the idea hasn't come to them just now for the first time. They have probably been thinking about it for years, but they just never found a way to get it done. The idea of locking themselves away for endless hours and doing the work themselves never appealed, and perhaps they never met anyone who had a process that would make only a small imprint on their schedule.

At least, until we met.

I was extremely excited when I got a fax (I told you it was back in the day) from the tech mogul's assistant saying my proposal had been accepted and that I had gotten the job. I had visions of myself hanging out with my billionaire in the back of his Gulfstream, sipping champagne, and having the kind of leisurely conversations that I could brag about to my friends (without mentioning his name, due to confidentiality concerns, of course), that would ultimately lead to a brilliant, brilliant book. That is when I learned how busy billionaires are. And that is when I developed my process, which I have now used to create countless books over the years.

We start off by avoiding the initial mistake that most writers make, which is to focus on what the book needs to be about. This is a fatal error that practically every writer makes, but it seems so obvious. If we are going to write a book, don't we start with what we are going to put in the book?

No.

I will say it again, no. Definitely not.

Instead, we first decide on the core audience for the book. *That* is the real starting point.

Think of a target at a shooting range. There's a bull's eye surrounded by increasingly large concentric circles. The bull's eye in our case is the specific core audience for whom the book is meant. *A book is a tool of influence.* That sentence is so important I will repeat it: *A book is a tool of influence.* So the starting point for a successful book is not "What do we put in the book?" it is "Whom are we trying to influence?"

Maybe it is friends and family, in the case of a memoir. Maybe it is potential clients, investors, new hires, legislators, or other stakeholders. Maybe it is others in your field, and you want them to grasp and apply your way of thinking about problems. There may be multiple audiences—those are the concentric circles around the bull's eye. Those people are welcome to read the book and benefit from it, but the starting point for any book is the simple question: Who is in the bull's eye? Who exactly are we trying to influence?

You cannot write a successful book if you don't start with that question in mind.

Then you ask, where are those people now, and where do you want to take them? A book makes a case for a certain way of thinking, a certain way of acting. The lives of the readers—their business lives, their personal lives, their spiritual lives—whatever the topic—will be better if they follow your guidance. So where are they now ... and where do you want to take them?

Only once we have identified the core audience for the book, where they are now, and where you want them to go, can we begin to discuss contents for the book. Any successful person could probably write a dozen different books right now. I like to say, which book will give you CPR? CPR, of course stands for Cash in your Pocket ... Right now. That is my kind of CPR! Or if you are not writing the book to make money, what outcome do you want? Out of all the possible books you could write, *that* is the book to write right now.

So now we have identified the audience, where they are, and where they want to go. I will then ask what I call the Oprah question, which is this:

"Hi! I'm Oprah. Welcome to the show! Tell the audience why you wrote the book."

I've got to tell you, everybody loves this Oprah question. For years, while Oprah had her talk show, it was the dream of countless of my clients to make it to her couch (some did, I'm excited to report. You get a book … and you get a book … and so on). But there is something magical about Oprah. She represents the pinnacle of success for authors, and at the same time, she has been considered the premier interviewer for decades. Prince Harry and Meghan talked to Oprah first. So, the idea of going on Oprah's show, triggered by my Oprah question, puts readers in a very happy, almost trance-like state.

They just relax. I can see their shoulders dropping if we meet in person or on a Zoom call. They begin to ask themselves, why am I doing this? And their answers become the foundation of the table of contents for the book. Let me explain. For the next hour or so, I'm just sitting back and letting the client do most of the talking. I've asked the most critical question a writer could possibly ask a client—why did you write this book? The fact that it is in the past tense takes some of the tension out of the process because the client is coming from a place of the work already being complete. What a relief! It is already done; I didn't have to do anything! What fun!

So now the client talks, and I'm listening for potential chapter ideas. The call is recorded, of course, but I'm taking notes feverishly and organizing a table of contents on the fly, which I will then polish over the next couple of days and present to the client typically within 48 hours of the call. My goal at this point is to listen for a potential title, subtitle, chapter titles, and a paragraph or two of description that will explain what goes into each chapter.

We are creating what I call an itinerary for the journey. If you ever backpacked across Europe, you might have planned to spend three days in London, three days in Paris, three days in Geneva … and then you met someone in Paris, and the two of you went to Spain. Boom. It is the same thing with a book. The table of contents can and will be adjusted over the course of the writing. That is fine. It is just that both of us—the client and I—need to see, on paper, a clear sense of the flow of information from the author (the client) to the reader. That is what the table of contents is for. We will sign off on the table of contents in a second, typically much shorter call, and then get into the interviewing.

I mentioned earlier that the typical approach for writers is to do big stream-of-consciousness interviews with their clients and hope that a book somehow emerges from the mist. And as I've said, great books typically don't materialize from this process. Instead, a jumble of thinking that has no benefit to the client or to readers is usually what emerges. There is a better way, which I developed back when I worked with the first of my billionaire clients, the tech mogul I mentioned a moment ago.

I need one hour of interview time for each chapter. In that hour, the client and I will have a broad-based conversation that I will lead with open questions. Typically, I may not have to ask more than six or eight questions over the course of the hour. I just want the client to download everything in her head about the topic without concern for what goes in front of what, where stories are needed, and so on. Some of that can be filled in later. I just want the client to talk.

At the end of the first hour of interviewing, I explain that every hour of interviewing I do leads to 12 to 15 pages of the book. I explain they will have the chapter within two weeks of the call, and at that point, I will be expecting comments, like "I like this, I hate that, that doesn't sound like me, that is great, do more of this, do less of that," and so on. If I waited until the manuscript was done, I would be making a terrible mistake. I wouldn't be giving the client a chance to correct the material immediately. Since I deliver the chapter within two weeks of the call, I can present the remainder of the chapters to the client in what would be a second or third draft. This saves everyone—the client and me—enormous time and effort. Delivering chapters one at a time, and getting comments from the client, allows me to edit that chapter and then do the rest with what I've learned about their guidance regarding word choice, sentence structure, and so on.

I also warn my client, as that first hour ends, that they will probably go into a state of panic once we get off the call. Accomplished people are used to accomplishing things. Typically, in an hour, a highly successful person will have answered 20 e-mails, closed a deal, reached out to a prospect, met a patient, created a financial plan, ordered labs, or done something else tangible. Here, they can panic (we just talked for an hour! Nothing happened! What on earth?). I warn them that is how they are going to feel, and that the relief will only come when they get the first chapter in their inbox. This way, they can head off some of that sense of panic (although typically not all of it). And then they get the first chapter, and they see how I transformed that conversation into a solid, exciting, enticing first chapter of their book, and now they can trust the process.

And then it is wash, rinse, repeat, through the end of the book.

Research? Yeah, I've got people who can do research and get us specific facts and figures, but as I advise my clients, what will matter most to the reader is what is in the client's brain already. It is the client's work or life experience that will make the difference, and statistics will just buttress the conclusions that the client has already reached.

Some clients are very modest and don't really believe that they have a book in them, so I put it this way:

"I understand that a book sounds daunting; however, what if we thought of it as ten or twelve conversations, one for each chapter, about the things that matter most to you, about the ways you serve people, about the ways you run your business or your practice, or about how you think about your field? Couldn't we have ten or twelve interesting one-hour conversations about ten or twelve topics related to what you do?"

At that point, most of them shrug and say, "You are probably right." And then, they find that they really enjoy the interview process, because they have never been listened to in this way, and they have never had a chance to clarify their thinking. This is an incredibly important point, so let's pause and go more deeply into it. We live in a world where practically no one listens. Indeed, conversations these days amount to two people standing next to each other, or on a Zoom call or a phone call, essentially formulating what they are going to say and waiting for the other person to stop talking so that they can say what they want to say next. There is practically no listening today; wouldn't you agree?

When you get home from work, how much interest does your spouse or partner truly have in what you did today? It is limited, let's be honest. They are glad you had a good day at the office, but they have got their own stuff going on. Do they really want to sit down with you for an hour and just listen to everything you think regarding a specific topic that is part of your work life, or an earlier chapter in your personal history if you are doing a memoir? That is a big lift for even the most dedicated of spouses or partners. The short of it is that most of us go through our lives, and no one is listening to us.

Sometimes, people ask whether I consider AI a threat to what I do. I don't. Not in the least. That is because whatever AI is good for, it cannot listen to what you are saying and realize that there is something you want to say but you aren't quite saying, something that is incredibly important to you, and that something is what no one else in your field is saying. How do I know that no one else in your field is making that critical point? Because I've read everything else that has been written in your field. I'm a bookstore and library nerd. I've been in bookstores and libraries on average twice a week since I was 12 years old. And if I haven't read the key books in your field, I may well have written them! So, I'm listening for what you are saying that no one else in your field is saying. I'm listening for what you are saying that is so important to you that you might not even express the idea fully, for fear of being rejected or ridiculed. That is my gift, the ability to hear what is behind your thinking, to stop the presses and say, "Wait! What did you just say? Can we just talk a little more about that?"

When that happens, half the time, clients are surprised. They figure that "everybody knows" what they know or what they think. That is so not true! (Pardon the grammar, but that is how I felt, so that is how it is staying.) Why is it so not true? Most people are very humble about their thinking, even people who are arrogant about everything else. They figure that if they know something, everybody knows it. If they are thinking something, everybody is thinking it. And what really makes them so successful is the fact that no one else is thinking those thoughts. No one else has those ideas. Only they have those thoughts, and they don't even recognize just how breathtaking, different, and potentially earth-shaking they are for readers. So, it is my job to listen and listen and listen, and then when I hear one of those extraordinary ideas mentioned, either in part or in full, pull the red cord and say, "Stop! Let's talk this through!"

I belong to an entrepreneurship training program called The Strategic Coach®, led by Dan Sullivan. It is a brilliant program, and I cannot say enough good about it. I've been a part of the program for 20 years. One thing that Dan teaches is that every person has a Unique Ability®, and that we should identify our Unique Ability® and spend as much time as we possibly can just working in our Unique Ability®. Others say, get better at your weakness. Not Dan. He says that you should delegate the things you are bad at and even the things you are excellent at if they are not your Unique Ability® because those tasks are probably someone else's Unique Ability®.

I went through the extremely thoughtful process Strategic Coach® offers for identifying Unique Ability® many years ago. As I did so, I thought to myself, this is a waste of time. My Unique Ability® is writing. Why am I doing this? Wrong. My Unique Ability® turned out to be listening. A lot of people are terrific writers. Few people are terrific listeners. And for me, it is not just listening. It is listening with love. That is my unique ability—to listen with love. To listen without boredom, without envy, with total concentration and focus. That is the gift I bring my clients. That is something they typically don't experience at work or at home.

And they love it.

As a result, the books my team and I create are, if I may be allowed a moment of immodesty, a million times better than practically anybody else's books, because they are rooted in deep listening—listening with love—to what the client has to say. That, above all things, is what I bring to the table.

Okay, that was a bit boastful, but as the expression goes, it ain't braggin' if you can back it up. Let's talk about a related topic—the question of just how much an author (you) should talk about yourself in your book. Here's what I tell my clients:

People don't read books. It is so shocking that I will say it again: *People don't read books*. Instead, people use a book as a screenplay for a movie that is going to play in their head. In that movie, they play two people. They play themselves as student, and they play the role of you, the author, as teacher.

Isn't that interesting? I think it is! The point is that when they are being you in that movie, they need to know just enough about you so they can play the role of you effectively. If you are overly humble and modest and you don't say enough about yourself, the reader will feel bewildered. And if you talk too much about yourself, the reader will be bored (oh my gosh! Stop talking about yourself already! I know who you are!).

So it is my job to help the client find the sweet spot between saying too little and saying too much about themself. You can call it a Goldilocks zone kind of thing. And by the way, Chapter 1 is never about the author, and it is never about the history of the topic. Instead, Chapter 1 is typically about the problem the reader faces that this book will solve. I will say that again because it is so important: The goal of Chapter 1 is to lay out the problem or problems the reader faces that this book will solve for them. The hero of the journey is not the author; it is the reader!

The reader doesn't care a whit about the author until the reader knows the author understands the problems the reader is facing better than anyone on earth. So, unless we are talking about a memoir, which is a slightly different animal, typically, in Chapter 1, we focus on the problems the reader faces that the author most enjoys solving. At that point, the reader looks up and says, "Wow! This author has been reading my mail! This author really gets me! Who is this person?"

And then comes Chapter 2, which typically tells the author's story. Great! Now it is time to provide the reader with the information necessary so that when she is playing you in the movie in her head, she knows exactly who she is being at the moment when she is being you. And then comes the rest of the book, which is either your process, or your story, or your thinking about a given topic. And that is how we get it done.

Let me be clear. There are a lot of really outstanding ghostwriters in the world, and they do things differently from how I do them. And that is fine. I'm simply providing you my methodology, which has been proven successful over more than 1,000 books that my team and I have done over 35 years. If you are a writer, you are most welcome to adopt any or all the ideas I described in this chapter, from the process of selling through the process of getting a book done. And if you are thinking about getting a book done, well, I hope I've made my process clear and attractive. It has worked for a lot of other people so I have a fair amount of certainty when I claim it will work for you, too.

CHAPTER 5

ONCE UPON A FABLE

Humans are wired to love stories, because the stories we tell ourselves explain life to us and make us feel safe. This has been true ever since man sat around the campfire after a long day's hunt, interpreting experiences and remembering the days of old.

Today, instead of sitting around a fire, we stare into screens, but it is the same thing. We are looking for people to tell stories that help us make sense of the world around us. Today, we call these stories "news" or "movies" or "shows." At the end of the day, stories are how humans connect with others and make the world safe.

So, it is not surprising that storytellers have important roles to play in society today, including in the business world. Stories are sticky. They remain in our minds long after facts and figures fade. Or, as I was advised at the beginning of my writing career, "No one remembers even a well-written government report."

I've been writing fables and novels for clients for as long as I can remember, and I love doing so. Some clients specify that they want stories told, whether in the form of a novel or business fable, which I will define in a moment. And sometimes, clients will explain the ideas they want to get across, and I will propose a fable as the ideal way of doing so. Let me explain.

We all know what a fable is, going back to Aesop and his story of the Tortoise and the Hare. Religious literature is replete with stories, which can be called parables or lessons. The beautiful thing about stories by any name is that they empower the reader to identify the lessons and teach themselves what is vital. If the Bible said, "Thou shalt not hide thy talents under a bushel," much of the resonance of the story about the talents would have been lost. Instead, readers read or hear the story of the individual who did not use his talents (then a measure of money, and now a measure of ability) was criticized. So we say to ourselves, "Wow! I don't want to be like that guy! I'm going to use my talents and get out there!" the lesson lands more strongly because, in effect, we are teaching it to ourselves.

In these pages, you will see several examples of fables I created for clients. In all the examples in this book, the clients did not come in with the idea of a fable. It is just that the lessons they wanted to convey to their audiences met two specific criteria:

1. There were already a ton of books on their subject, so writing yet another "Seven Steps to" or "Five Principles of" book would be redundant and boring.
2. They were only trying to teach a handful of key points.

If you are writing about real estate investing, or financial services, or for that matter, a variety of other topics from how to find the perfect mate to how to get divorced, you can search Amazon and find countless nonfiction books that give you step-by-step guides to accomplishing those goals.

How boring to write yet another one.

If you are doing a book that offers a lot of pieces of information and guidance, then a fable is probably not going to be the play. I will give you an example. I did a book recently for a tech CEO whose firm helps other tech companies manage their employees. Tech companies often come into existence when an engineer decides he wants to go off on his own, and then drives enough business to require the assistance of other techies. The problem is that managing techies is like herding cats, and the technologist CEO is typically more comfortable with zeros and ones than actual human beings. Hilarity does not ensue. Instead, you have got a big mess, where people who don't have great management or people skills are trying to manage other people who also don't necessarily have great people skills.

The book I did for my client offers several hundred different pieces of guidance about how to make a tech company run right and ensure that everyone from the CEO to the entry level hires are happy and marching in the same direction. That book would not work well as a fable; there is simply too much to teach. By contrast, if your message is limited to a few key takeaways, then you are a candidate for a fable, and I will tell you so. We will then talk about how the story should be structured, where it takes place, who our characters are, what is being taught, and why. It is a really fun and exciting process. I love it when clients trust me with the idea for a fable. We typically end up having a really great time.

I also ghostwrite novels, and I'm not the only one. There is a history in the publishing industry of fiction not being written by the purported author. Sometimes clients will come to me with an idea for a nonfiction book that they would like to write. They tell me the story, and I think to myself, wow, if you publish the story as you have described it, somebody is going to sue you, or somebody is going to come after you, and not for an autograph. So in those cases, I have counseled them to tell the story in fictional form, so as to avoid libel lawsuits or worse.

One such client came to me a dozen years ago with a remarkable story to tell. His wife's great-grandfather had invented a device which, a century later, remains a staple in the production of a common household item. Pardon my being vague, but I'm bound by confidentiality rules, and I also don't want anybody coming after me!

It turned out that the brother-in-law running the company that held rights to that still much-desired device was sweeping anywhere between $40 million and $100 million off the table. My client wanted to write an exposé about how evil his brother-in-law was.

The more he told me about his brother-in-law, the more I cautioned him that writing a non-fiction book may be detrimental to his health. Instead, I suggested that we do a novel that told the story of an individual who had committed the same kinds of alleged crimes as his brother-in-law, but in a business arena far removed from the actual one. I also suggested that, given everything he told me about his brother-in-law, the likelihood that he would survive much longer after publication day was limited. So, we went the novel route. He was happy, and, as far as I know, still alive. Whether the brother-in-law has ever been brought to justice is beyond my pay grade.

A client came to me with a similar story about shenanigans in a financial services firm. My client wanted to do an exposé because he was angry at the people who were behaving so fraudulently. Instead, I suggested that he either write an anonymous letter to the SEC or just stay out of the actual case and write a novel that, along the same lines as the previous story I shared, told the same story but in a very oblique way. He agreed, and the novel ended up being a best seller that became the foundation of a network series.

Fiction saves lives.

So, whether you are looking to make a score, settle scores, or simply convey lessons to people in your audience, fables and fiction can be wonderful ways to go.

CHAPTER 6

BOOK MARKETING: BUYER BEWARE!

I want you to be really careful if you are going to put serious money into a book marketing campaign. There are some awesome book marketing people out there. I know who they are, so drop me an e-mail (michaellevinwrites@gmail.com), and I will let you know who is great, depending on what you are trying to accomplish. The most important thing I can say about spending money on book marketing is *proceed with caution.*

There is more disappointment around book marketing than practically any other aspect of getting a book done. Some of it is just plain silly. If you spend $10 on book marketing, you will not be sitting next to Oprah next Tuesday on a special. Let's get real. But it is more than that. As I say elsewhere in these pages, one of the hardest things to do in the world is sell copies of your book to strangers. Authors can spend tens of thousands of dollars on book marketing, but if they don't do it carefully and intentionally, they may have very little to show for their investment of time, money, and hope.

The criteria for choosing book marketers are fairly similar to what I suggested regarding choosing a ghostwriter. Is the website professional? Are there blurbs from happy clients whose goals were achieved by the campaigns the book marketer created? Do they do tons of different kinds of marketing, and also happen to do book marketing, or do they specialize? (Go with a specialist.)

If you are going to spend money on a campaign, understand there is often a fundamental mismatch between what you want (book sales, the cash register ringing, speaking engagements, what have you) and what the book marketer views as success.

Many book marketers use what are called "impressions" as their measuring stick. Let's say they get an opinion piece you wrote, or that they wrote for you, in USA Today. And let's say, for the sake of argument, that USA Today has a circulation of one million. This means the book marketer will proudly tell you that you received one million impressions. What does that mean, exactly? Did a million people read your article?

Doubtful. Of the people who did read your article, how many people noticed at the bottom that you are the author of a particular book and then went to Amazon to buy it? Maybe none. So, don't be seduced by how many impressions you get. Instead, have a conversation with the book marketer before you write a check and ask, "How do you measure success? Is it impressions? Because I can't put impressions on a deposit slip."

Next, while there are some outstanding, high-integrity book marketers in the world, by and large, and I hate saying anything negative, there are a whole lot of scoundrels in this field. They see first-time authors coming and they take full advantage. They promise the moon, cash, or check, and then you never see them or hear from them again until it is time for them to collect the next install- ment. Recently, a book marketer I have known and trusted for de- cades went to a client I had referred to her behind my back and sold him a $25,000 virtual book tour, which sold *exactly zero books*. I was shocked and outraged that she had done this. It was an unscrupu- lous, immoral thing to do, compounded by the fact that she didn't even mention it to me first, and I was paying her for the client's book marketing. If you can't trust the people you have known forever, then whom can you trust?

I referred a different client who was working on a series of children's books to one of the top brand-name marketing companies in New York. The person they assigned to the campaign botched it. The owner of the company did practically nothing to make things up to the client and then, somehow, decided to blame me. She hasn't taken my calls since.

Sigh.

The short of it is that if you aren't going to thoroughly vet a book marketer, don't hire them. Ask if you can speak with past clients who have books in your genre. If you wrote a novel, don't speak to their nonfiction clients. Nonfiction is a million times easier to market than fiction. A nonfiction author goes on Oprah. Oprah says, "Tell the audience why you wrote the book." The author says, "I wanted to share my three-step process to finding the right partner, raising kids, whatever."

Oprah asks the same question to a novelist: "Tell the audience why you wrote the book." The novelist goes wide-eyed, scratches his chin, and says, "Wow! I never thought of that! That's a really great question!"

And Oprah cuts in, saying, "We will be back after this commercial but with a different guest."

If you try to promote a novel, make sure that your book marketer has successfully promoted other novels prior to yours. Don't be the guinea pig. And if the book marketer cannot or will not share names and contact information of happy past clients in your genre, move on.

I frequently advise my clients to skip the book marketing expense initially and do things in a cheap and dirty, yet highly effective, manner. I owe the concept to the late Chet Holmes, a leading sales trainer and author who counseled his followers to create a "Dream 100." Your Dream 100 consists of the 100 people you would most like to work with. Identify them. Get their physical addresses. Mail them a book with a personal, handwritten note explaining why you are sending them the book and how you would like to serve them, partner with them, or whatever you have in mind. You can put 100 books in 100 envelopes with handwritten notes for under $1,000. You won't get all your Dream 100 … but you will get some. And then, peel off some of the money you make because of those relationships and invest it in a book marketing campaign *with a marketer you have carefully vetted, as above.*

The Dream 100 is a really exciting and fun way to expand your horizons because you have to start thinking about all the people out there in the world with whom you would like to work. Aim high! If you are thinking of them, they just might be thinking about a gap that only you can fill. Where is the harm? This is why I suggest you start with a Dream 100 instead of doing a major book marketing campaign from the start.

The movie studios say that it takes eight impressions before someone is ready to go see or download a particular movie. An impression, in this case, might be a bus ad, an ad they see on a website, a favorable mention from a friend, a review they read somewhere, and so on. If it takes a movie eight impressions before you are willing to see it, how many impressions do you think it will take before someone is ready to buy your book? Are you prepared to spend all the money it takes to have your ad on buses, to garner reviews, to do podcasts, and so on, to get to that magic figure of eight impressions? Doesn't that sound like a huge lift? That is what you are up against. And remember, when you are trying to sell books to strangers, you are competing with all the uses of their discretionary income and time. They could buy some other book or no book at all. They could just watch some *Seinfeld* reruns or get lost on social media. They could take a nap. People could do a thousand things with their time that, unfortunately, have nothing to do with buying and reading your book.

Cutting through the clutter and getting people to focus on your specific offering … and then getting them to put down their credit card to buy your book? I don't mean any disrespect to you or to your book. You are awesome, and your book is fantastic! It is just that getting other people to recognize that is difficult and expensive. And all too often, for first-time authors, as my mother would have said, it ends in tears. Start with the Dream 100. Put your book on your website front and center so the first thing people see is your smiling face on the cover of your book. Let people download it for free as a PDF in exchange for an e-mail address. Put it in the signature line of your e-mails so people can download the PDF just by clicking. The important thing is to get your ideas out there. Selling copies is secondary.

The only exception to this rule is that when you speak, you can sell tons of copies at the back of the room. You will just have somebody there with a credit card thingamabob attached to an iPhone, or people can Venmo or Zelle the money. Modern times! Very exciting! In this case, you are printing the book for $3 and selling it for $30. That is good math. No book publicist necessary.

If you are still interested in finding a top book publicist to get attention for your book, I'll recommend 3. First, Keith Gainsboro and his outstanding firm Elevate (Elevatecom.com). For promoting fiction, Javier Perez at Page-Turner Publicity (pgturnerpub@aol. com), and for television coverage, Mike Levenstein (no relation!) at Levensteinmedia.com.

So now you know pretty much everything I know about creating, publishing, and marketing books. Now let me tell you some stories about some of the books I've helped bring into the world.

THE STORIES BEHIND THE BOOKS

SECTION 1

FABLES

GARY R. MILLER

Taming Chaos: A Parable on Decision Making

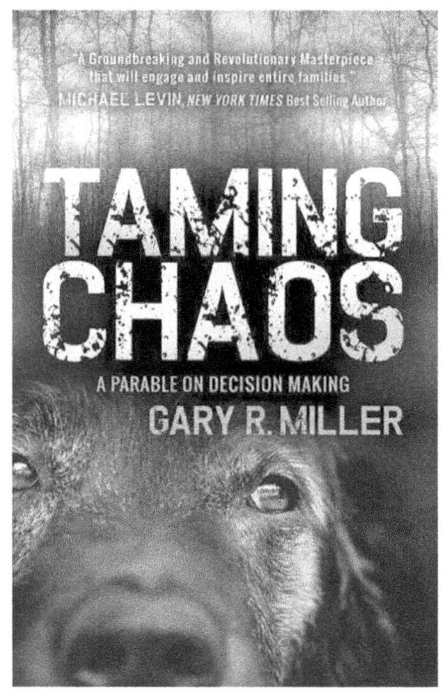

Gary Miller is a highly successful insurance professional running a third-generation family firm in Spring House, Pennsylvania. He didn't want a book to drive business—he had all the business he could handle—but instead, he wanted to get a passion project across. He wanted to teach teenagers how to assess risk.

Teenagers, Gary believes, minimize risks because their brains aren't fully formed, and, well, they are teenagers, so they do stupid, reckless things. Mostly, they get away with those insane choices. Sometimes, however, they don't.

Conversely, Gary points out, teens can be overly risk-averse and miss out on opportunities for growth or happiness. Maybe they won't try out for the school play or the football team or ask that girl or boy to prom. And then they have to live with the disappointment and frustration over "what could have been."

Measuring risk is what Gary, and his father and grandfather, spent their careers doing. That is what insurance is all about - making good bets based on the likelihood of success. But teenagers are different animals, and I suggested to Gary that instead of doing a nonfiction book that presented risk assessment in a series of modules or anything else kids might find boring, we tell a story.

Everybody loves stories, or fables, if you will because fables empower the reader to pull out the moral of the story for themselves. Nobody likes to be told "thou shalt" or "thou shalt not." On the other hand, if there is a story, and you can see the consequences that occurred to the person in the story, you and you alone have the power to decide what the lesson is and whether you should apply it to yourself. That is why people like stories. On top of that, they are easier to remember. Tony Robbins spends about an hour in his Business Mastery seminars teaching three simple points - "It is out there, it is worth it, and I'm gonna go get it." It sounds easy to remember, right? It is also really easy to forget.

So instead, Tony tells the story of an individual who was convinced that he had identified the location of a Spanish galleon that had sunk centuries earlier and had been lying on the ocean floor ever since with its cargo holds bulging with gold. Tony takes his audience through this individual's years of trying to put a crew together, test dives, finally finding it, bringing it to the surface, and enjoying the bounty - even though it took him 16 years. When you learn the concept of "it's out there, it is worth it, and I'm gonna go get it" in the context of this story, you are not likely to forget that lesson.

Back to Gary. I suggested that we have a story about a brother and sister who are walking to school. It is the first day of the new school year, always fraught for kids, and they come across a German Shepherd that has been hit by a car. Of course, the kids want to take the dog home and nurture him and have a pet they can care for and love. So, here comes the risk assessment part: Is the dog likely to live? Was he tame or wild before the accident? How will he be if he recovers? Is that a dog you want in the house with children?

Gary loved the idea, and we wrote a fable called Taming Chaos, with Chaos being the name of the dog in the story. Spoiler alert: the kids brought the dog home, and everything worked out. Gary has used this book for years to go into high schools and teach kids about proper risk assessment. Would it have been as successful if he had been teaching four modules or six chapters or anything grownup and boring like that?

This is a story, albeit a true story, so instead of telling you the moral of the story, I will assume that you will have figured it out for yourself.

MATT REINER

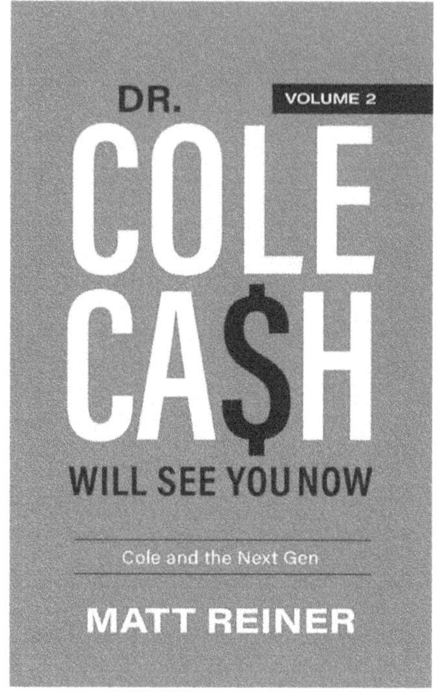

Dr. Cole Cash Will See You Now: Cole and the Next Gen

Follow me on this one. Matt Reiner is a consultant who works solely with financial advisors, helping them understand their issues about money so that they can help their clients identify and understand *their* issues about money. So how do you turn a practice like that into a book that his market will want to read?

As you know, I'm a big believer in stories to illustrate ideas. In this case, I thought, what if we had a psychologist who found money interesting but who found people with psychological issues not that interesting? He is from a small town in the South, first to college, first to grad school, and had never heard of a financial advisor in his life until he met a woman at college who was planning on becoming just that. Fascinated, he decides that he is going to become a therapist or counselor … just to financial advisors. And he is going to help them identify and handle their issues regarding money so they can help their clients identify and handle their issues with money.

Anyway, thanks to Matt's trust in his somewhat wacky writer (me), a new character was born, Dr. Cole Cash, and he is the centerpiece of a series of books that I did with John, the first of which is called *Dr. Cole Cash Will See You Now*. Each book presents four "clients" - financial advisors who are seeing Dr. Cash to work out certain issues around money. Each of the four issues presented in each book is something financial advisors deal with every day. Dr. Cash has a waiting room, a couch, and a comfy chair … all the accoutrements of a practicing psychologist, which is exactly what he is. He can help his clients with precisely the issues with which John helps his financial advisor clients.

And a good time is had by all.

I always hold my breath when I present an idea like Dr. Cole Cash to a client. Will they think I am crazy? Is the idea any good? Will they go for it? So, it is always very satisfying when a client runs with the idea, and it is even more satisfying when the published book comes out and helps people. Not a bad day at the office if you ask me.

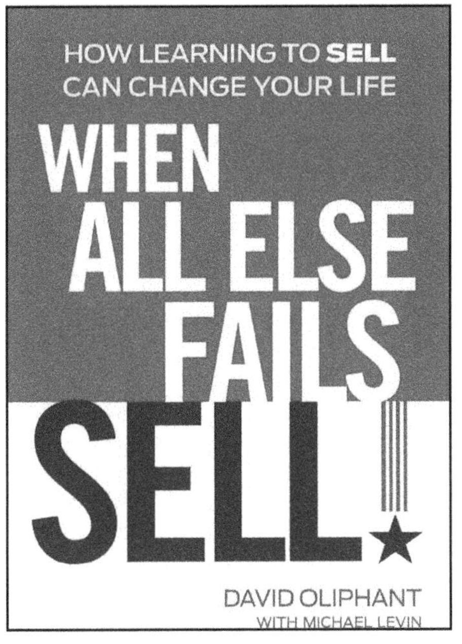

DAVID OLIPHANT

*When All Else Fails, Sell!:
How Learning to Sell Can
Change Your Life*

David Oliphant wasn't happy. An inveterate salesman who was responsible for moving more than a billion dollars' worth of rare coins, supplements, books, and other items on QVC, David found two things deeply troubling. First, the profession of sales commanded little respect in American society. People tended to associate sales professionals primarily with used car salesmen, people who would say or do anything to close a deal that was bad for the customer.

On top of that, David was deeply troubled by the fact that countless veterans were returning from service overseas, particularly from the Gulf Wars and Afghanistan, unable to translate their military experience into the ability to make a living.

He wanted to do a book that would raise the profile of selling as a career and make it particularly applicable and interesting to returning veterans. When he laid out the problem the book was meant to solve, I proposed that we write a story (imagine that!). We would focus on a vet coming out of the military with all the skills that the business world prizes and little understanding of a place he could find in the business world. In other words, it is a story about a veteran who learned to take his leadership, communication, courage, and cooperative skills, which he had gained in the military, and turn them into a highly successful sales career.

David believes that the same mindset that it takes to succeed in the military - that same constellation of character traits I just mentioned - is precisely what it takes to succeed as a top sales professional. So the book was about elevating the profile of sales while at the same time making it intriguing and accessible to veterans, who A) needed to make a living and B) could potentially be great at doing just this.

Readers Digest Press recognized the value in carrying this message to ex-military, soon-to-be ex-military, and employers who needed to be educated as to the extraordinary value that our veterans can bring to the business world. They published the book, and I'm happy to say that generations of veterans have found great careers for themselves, selling honestly and nobly. Nothing to do with used car salesmen or flashy suits. And at the same time, the business world has tapped into a cadre of highly trained, disciplined, hard-working men and women who have added in meaningful ways, and always with integrity, to their bottom line.

Hooah!

# SECTION 2
BUSINESS

GARY KADI

Million Dollar Dentistry

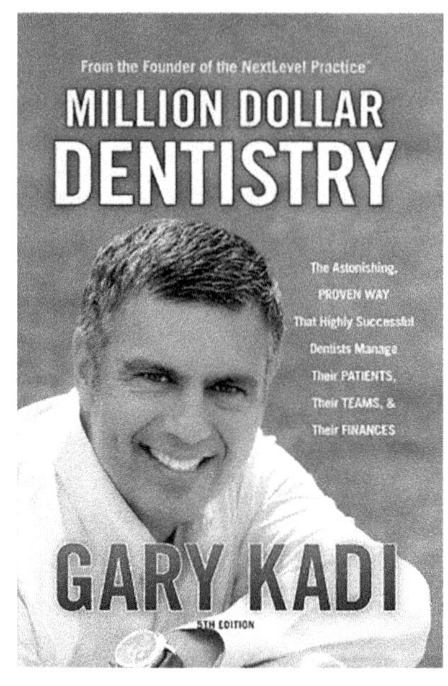

Gary came to me almost 20 years ago with a plan for a consultancy that would serve dentists, a group Gary had identified as being in deep need of better professional guidance. Many dentists were floundering, and their businesses were failing. While they might have been great chair side, they had little idea of how to run a dental practice as a thriving business.

He came to me and said, "I want to get five dentists to pay me $120,000 each to consult with their practices for a year. I'm going to promise them dollar-for-dollar returns, so they are not risking a penny. This way, I will make $600,000 a year, and only five people will have my cell phone number."

So, we set about writing *Million Dollar Dentistry*, which has now sold more than 60,000 copies.

After the book came out, one of the three leading providers of dental equipment came to Gary and said, "We loved your book. We want to send you around the country and have you speak to audiences of dental office teams at Ritz-Carltons. We will pay for your travel expenses, and we will pay you $6,000 a pop for each talk. All we ask is that, over the course of the talk, you say something nice about us."

Gary went on the road and galvanized his audiences with his unique thinking about how to run a dental practice like a business. He very quickly outstripped his initial dream of finding five clients to serve. Instead, he built a consultancy that served thousands of dentists, which he had recently sold to his team. Moreover, Gary is in the process of rolling up his top 20 dental practice clients into a single entity that he now runs. I have since done book after book with Gary, including one about the question of "deserve level."

Most medical doctors, he points out, come from families of physicians, for whom entering medicine is a family tradition. By contrast, many dentists come from blue-collar backgrounds, and they are the first in their families to attend college or a professional school. As a result, dentists sometimes feel as though they are "less than" when compared with their M.D. brethren. Gary's mission has been not just to improve the quality of individual dental practices but to raise the level of self-respect of the dental industry in its entirety. These days, you see your dentist for a lot longer than you see your primary care physician and top dentists doing things Gary's way net seven figures annually. Thanks to Gary, dentists no longer have to feel that they are second class when they are contemplating their medical school colleagues.

VALERIE ROMLEY

Beyond Translation: The Marketer's Field Guide to Understanding Today's Transcultural Consumer

As globalization marches on, more and more companies want to appeal to broader markets, domestic and foreign. It sounds easy enough, right? You've got a successful brand or ad campaign here in the United States, why can't you just translate it to other countries and other cul-

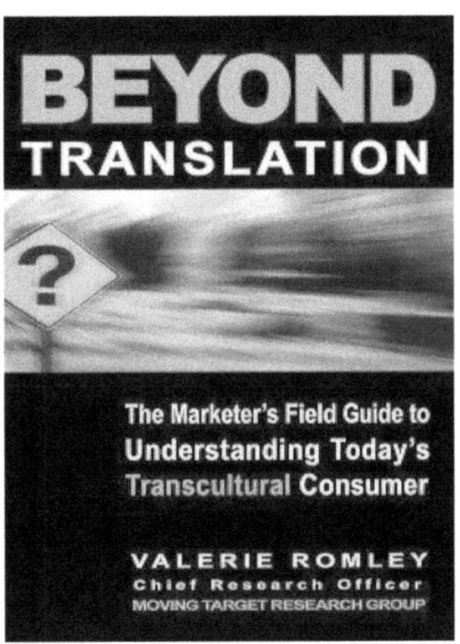

tures and watch your profits soar?

Not so fast, Valerie Romley counsels her clients, as well as her readers, in *Beyond Translation*, which I had the privilege to edit. She points out that you can't just sell to people whose ethnicity or nation of origin is different from your own. You have got to understand who they really are, and how they differ culturally from the markets you have traditionally favored.

She brings a few hilarious examples of American companies that got it dead wrong when they tried to take their brands or ad campaigns to Mexico. Remember the Chevy Nova? Nova might sound like a neat name for a car in the United States. In Mexico, not so much because "no va" in Spanish means "doesn't go." Or what about the ubiquitous "Got milk?" campaign that was a staple of seemingly every highway billboard or magazine ad for years? Once again, marketers swung and missed when they took the "Got milk?" concept to Mexico. That is because the way they wrote "Got milk" in Spanish translated to … and you cannot make this stuff up … "Are you lactating?"

Valerie was fascinated by cultural differences after having lived and traveled abroad. She built her consultancy around South Asian, Latino, and East Asian communities. Her book guides readers on how to enter those markets around the world and how to understand individuals and communities from those regions who had come to settle here in the United States.

You would think that entities as big as GM or the Milk Board, or whoever sponsors the "Got milk?" campaign, would have had enough common sense to research these basic linguistic concepts before they spent millions, or tens of millions, embarrassing themselves for no reason when they took "no va" and "Are you lactating?" to Mexican consumers.

Alas, you would have been wrong. Valerie Romley to the rescue.

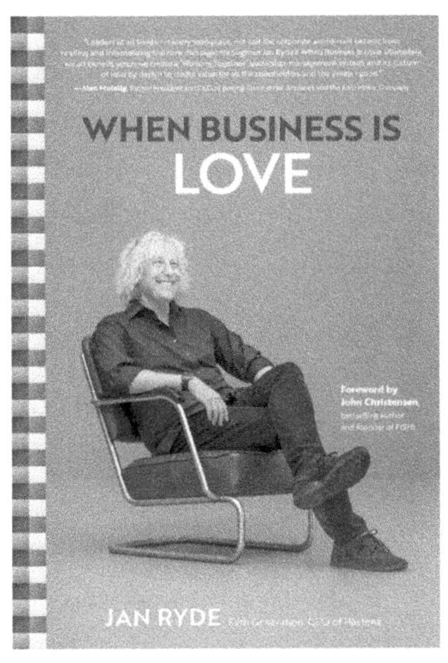

JAN RYDE, FIFTH GENERATION CEO, HÄSTENS

When Business is Love: The Spirit of Hästens—at Work, at Play, and Everywhere in Your Life

A century and a half ago, a Swedish saddle maker fell in love and moved to the town of Köping where his beloved resided, and re-established his saddlery there. Back then, your customers were your neighbors, so you had to deliver the highest level of mastery and quality if your business was to thrive. Around the turn of the century, that saddler's son recognized that horses were going out and cars were coming in. So, he took the skills that went into saddlery and started to make extraordinarily high-quality beds.

A century later, the Hästen brand stands for the same thing that the founder stood for a century and a half ago—mastery, quality, and a sense that they are making products not for strangers but for friends around the world. Hästens is famous for its Grand Vivitus bed, which retails for more than $750,000 and is a favorite of celebrities like Drake and Post Malone. At the same time, Hästen's beds, which are warrantied for 25 years and typically last twice to three times that long, sell from $10,000 and up. Hästen is the Swedish word for horse, which befits the company's origins and points to the fact that the beds are filled with the finest quality horsehair sourced from around the world. Horsehair provides a more restful night of sleep because it does not overheat or wear out. The handmade beds—the ones at price points below the Grand Vivitus—belong to celebrities, including Taylor Swift, Oprah Winfrey, Ellen DeGeneres,

Charlie Sheen, Brad Pitt, George Clooney, Maria Sharapova, and a host of others.

The fifth-generation CEO of the company, Jan Ryde, took over when it was in the doldrums a generation ago. A business school professor, he had concluded that the best way to run an enterprise was not on competition or fear but love. He promised himself that he would write a book about that philosophy when the company reached the $100 million sales level. *When Business is Love* is that book.

The book details the company's journey from its founder, the love-struck master saddler, through five generations of growth and service. *When Business is Love* breaks down the various components of Hästen's approach to business—mastery, love of people, quality, work, and so on—and offers a refreshingly positive outlook on how to build and serve. For me, one of the most fun things about working on the book was the chance to make repeated visits to Köping to tour the factory and to fluff the horsehair at the heart of every Hästen's bed. I sleep on a Hästen's, the T 2000, which retails for around $52,000.

It's worth it.

The author relaxing on a $750,000 Grand Vividus at Hastens'
showroom in Koping, Sweden

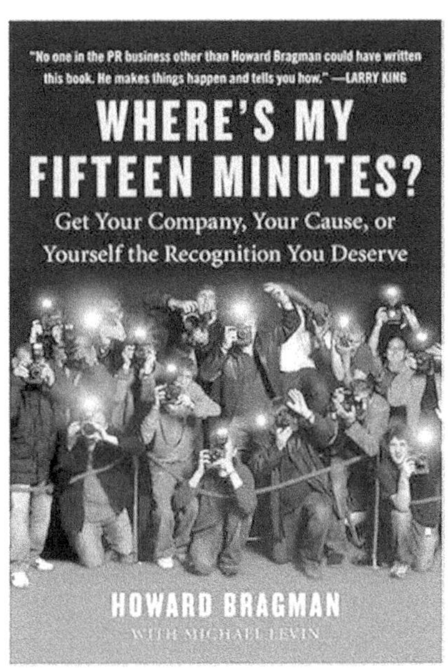

HOWARD BRAGMAN

Where's My Fifteen Minutes? - Get Your Company, Your Cause, or Yourself The Recognition You Deserve

Howard Bragman used to say he had the perfect name for his profession, PR. Bragman, get it? Bragging? They say it ain't braggin' if you can back it up, and Howard backed up his claim of being the top Hollywood publicist (okay, he would never have said that about himself) with a career that included clients from Frank Sinatra to Madonna to Coca-Cola to Monica Lewinsky. He also had a specialty in helping gay individuals come out, including John Amaechi, who became the first NBA player to go public with his homosexuality, and NFL prospect Michael Sam.

Howard wanted to do a book that shared with the world his techniques for gaining attention to worthy causes. Unless you were incredibly famous and impossibly rich, you couldn't afford to hire Howard's company, Fifteen Minutes, named, of course, after Andy Warhol's prediction that "In the future, we will all be famous for fifteen minutes." So, Howard wanted to write a book for the everyday person who needed to manage publicity in their lives.

Howard liked to say that PR didn't just stand for public relations - it stood for perception and reality. A great campaign could alter the perception of the reality of an individual or an entity. For the purposes of our book, we settled on a typical Main Street business, a mythical dry cleaner that was extremely earth-friendly in its approach to laundering clothing with an environmental flair.

Howard took the techniques he used for growing the reputation of a young Madonna and resuscitating the reputation of an even younger Monica Lewinsky and he showed how those tools could be used to publicize a small business.

Howard was a staple on CNN, but not every business needs CNN or national media to survive and thrive. Howard's methods, as revealed in the book, helped tens of thousands of individuals and business owners create "publicizable moments" for themselves and launch or grow their careers or businesses.

While I was putting this project together, I was shocked to discover that Howard had passed a year earlier. We did our book in 2006 and had remained in touch ever since. In the foreword to the book, Howard graciously thanked me for taking him, a first-time author, "from crayons to perfume," a line from the theme to the movie *The Prime of Miss Jean Brodie*. I loved Howard, and I loved learning from him. He is sorely missed.

HOWARD MAKLER

The Blueprint: How to Build a Wildly Successful Business … And Have a Blast While You're Doing it

Howard Makler thinks *Big*. That's Big with a B. He thinks in terms of billions, also with a B. In *The Blueprint*, which also conveniently starts with B, he shares what he has learned as a serial entrepreneur regarding the creation of billion-dollar businesses. Howard has been there and done that a few times, which makes him eminently qualified to dispense such advice. The book lays out a clear plan for envisioning and building out a billion-dollar, "blue ocean" business of one's own.

Howard's entrepreneurial career began as a teen when he started his first successful business. At one point, he realized he needed to be in touch with Steve Jobs, so he did what any self-respecting teenager would do — he picked up the phone and called Jobs. Not surprisingly, if you know Howard, he got through and gained entrepreneurial guidance from the master himself.

Edward DeBartolo and his family are famous real estate investors and former owners of the San Francisco 49ers. When Howard was setting up a real estate investment trust, he needed some advice. He called DeBartolo … and got through. That is what Howard does.

The idea behind *The Blueprint* is to offer entrepreneurs the precise steps one must take to build a business with a potential billion-dollar payday. He is extremely candid about his growth experiences and extremely generous with the wisdom he has derived from his multiple successful ventures. He indicates the mistakes many entrepreneurs make and shows how to avoid them. The book isn't theory; it's lived experience. It will save readers enormous time, money, and heartache on their entrepreneurial journeys. If you want to learn how to make not just some money but a lot of money while staying scrappy and having a great time, Howard is your man, and *The Blueprint* is your book.

DAVID FISHOF

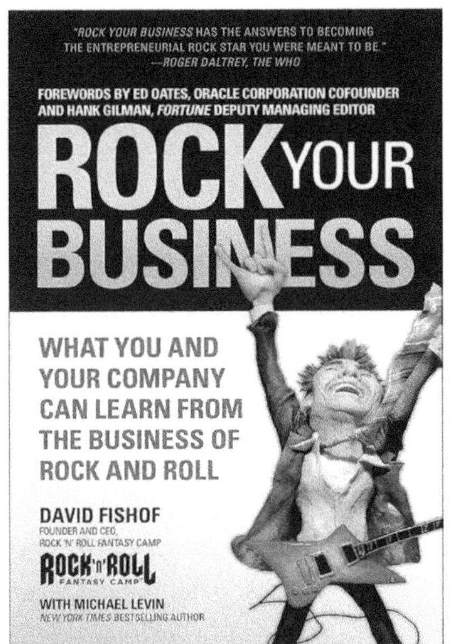

Rock Your Business: What You and Your Company Can Learn from the Business of Rock and Roll

David Fishof might be the most brilliantly original entrepreneur I have ever met. He wanted to work with Ringo Starr, so he went to Pepsi and told them that he could get Ringo Starr, but he needed a million dollars.

He got the million dollars.

Then he went to Ringo and said that he had a million dollars from Pepsi, and asked would Ringo be interested in creating a band of his own, comprising the highest caliber rock stars, for a tour?

Ringo said yes, and Ringo Starr and his All-Starr band was born. The band toured the world and was incredibly successful. People came up to David all the time and asked, "What was it like, being backstage with Ringo and all those amazing musicians?"

A new idea was born. There were fantasy camps for sports teams - middle-aged guys (and some gals) could write a big check and spend a few days in the dugout being coached by the Major League baseball players they had loved as kids. Why not do the same thing in music?

Why not, indeed? So, David created the Rock and Roll Fantasy Camp with counselors like Roger Daltry, Nils Lofgren, Alice Cooper, Tommy Lee, Rudy Sarzo, Slash, Dave Navarro, and Joe Walsh. Those are the counselors; the campers are doctors, lawyers, professionals, or anyone with three chords and a dream.

Rock Camp works this way - you spend three days or so rehearsing with a small band of fellow campers with one-on-one instruction from the counselors, who are the big-name folks mentioned above. Then, you perform with your band and your counselor at a top venue in Los Angeles or Las Vegas. Rock Camp became so successful that it now offers a comedy fantasy camp with Jay Leno, Adam Corolla, and others. In a world where successful people already own everything they could think of, this is one experience they may never have imagined.

Most of us don't recognize that the music business is one of the smartest and best-organized industries on the planet. David realized that he could teach the same skills he used to become a highly successful concert promoter so that other entrepreneurs could run their businesses more effectively. And that is how the book we did, *Rock Your Business!*, a number one Amazon business best seller, was born.

While working on the book with David, he invited my kids and me to a day at Rock and Roll Fantasy Camp. We weren't campers, just observers. One of the counselors that day was Joey Ramone. My kids were then ten, eight, and eight years old. We sat on a couch in a downstairs rehearsal room in a recording studio in North Hollywood, California, as Joey led his campers in a spirited rendition of *I Want to be Sedated*. My kids had no idea what they were experiencing, but I knew.

When they were done singing, I asked Joey if he would autograph the sheet music for my daughter's fifth-grade teacher. He kindly obliged. I told my daughter, "When you give this to your teacher, she is going to scream."

"Oh, daddy," my daughter replied. "She won't scream."

"Wait and see," I said.

Sure enough, she came home from school the next day wide-eyed, telling me, "You were right! She screamed!"

You can go to rockcamp.com and learn more about the camp experience, or you can read David's book. Either way, he will rock your world.

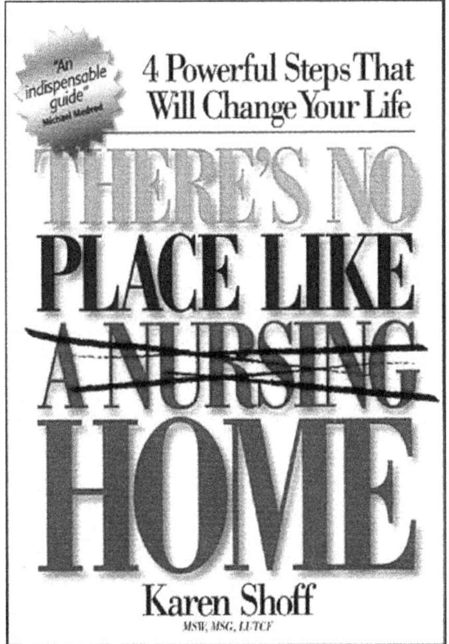

KAREN SHOFF

There's No Place Like A Nursing Home: 4 Powerful Steps That Will Change Your Life

Karen Shoff is a gerontologist who studies the best strategies for healthy aging and who developed a lifelong aversion to nursing homes. The idea of warehousing the elderly with substandard care and little family contact was abhorrent to her. A deeply religious person, Karen believed that our society was going off the rails by making it acceptable to abandon our elderly family members to a lonely and often premature death.

Karen realized that the key to keeping people out of nursing homes was to help them find the funding they needed to be able to be cared for in their own homes. She also learned that when you have an elderly couple, and one is caring for the other, the caregiver typically dies first. The emotional and physical strain of meeting the responsibilities of an aging spouse is simply too much for most people.

So Karen decided that the way she could help the most people while living true to her values was to become an insurance agent alongside her role as a gerontologist and focus on long-term care insurance or LTCI. Now, LTCI is an extremely complex product with a huge number of variables, and it typically takes a day and a half to explain to a prospect. On top of that, the product itself, at times, has been tainted in the marketplace due to shoddy companies that offered it and failed to live up to their agreements.

Karen discovered, to her dismay, that she could spend the requisite day and a half with a prospect, educate that individual as to all the ins and outs of LTCI, and help them understand that legitimate providers would stand by their agreements, only to hear them say, "Look, I appreciate everything you have done for me, but if I don't let my brother-in-law write the policy, my spouse will kill me."

We did a book called *There is no Place Like a Nursing Home.* The purpose of the book was to educate readers as to why it was essential for them to stay out of nursing homes and why it was possible for them to stay home and receive care from professionals - not just their spouse or children - and have an insurance company pay for the whole thing.

The book explains long-term care insurance as one element in the process of keeping oneself or one's loved ones out of nursing homes.

Within 90 days of the book's publication, Karen sold so much long-term care insurance that she became part of the Million Dollar Roundtable, an important measure of success in the insurance field.

And best of all, the brothers-in-law were no longer getting the business.

SECTION 3

YOUR BEST LIFE

EDWARD A. TAUB, M.D. AND DAVID OLIPHANT

Managing Your Stress In Today's World

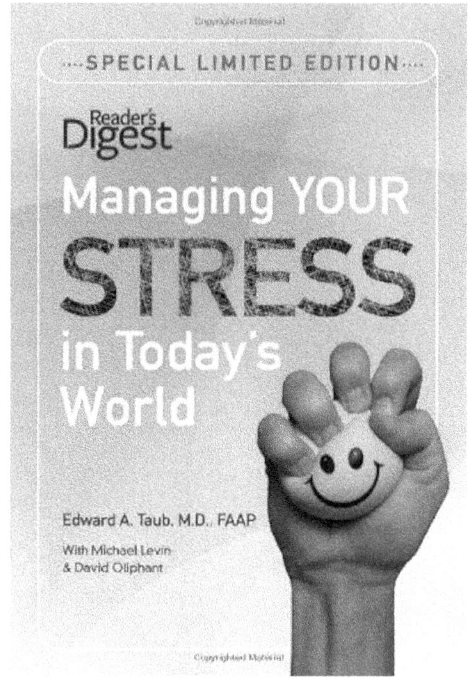

Over a 20-year span, David Oliphant sold more than a billion dollars' worth of collectibles, health products, and books to QVC's vast audience. *Readers Digest* came to QVC and said they wanted to do a book on stress reduction. Would I like to write the book along with a Dr. Edward Taub, an authority on the subject? The only stressful thing to think about was the window when the book could be sold on QVC was four weeks out. That left just one week to write the book, three weeks to publish it, and no margin of error.

I interviewed Dr. Taub over two days and then printed out my interview notes. I grabbed a chapter's worth of notes and my dictation device (this was before cell phones had audio recording apps), and I walked around my neighborhood, notes in hand, dictating chapters, one after the next. A day and a half later, a 150-page manuscript was complete.

The team at *Readers Digest* was phenomenal. They took the chapters with notes from my co-author and swiftly laid them out in book form, got a great cover design done, arranged for blurbs, and published the book on time so my co-author could go to QVC studios and pitch the book. It was a massive seller, and the audience could not have possibly known that four weeks prior, not one word of the book had been written.

MONTE WOOD AND NICOLE F. ROBERTS

Generosity Wins: How and Why this Game-Changing Superpower Drives our Success

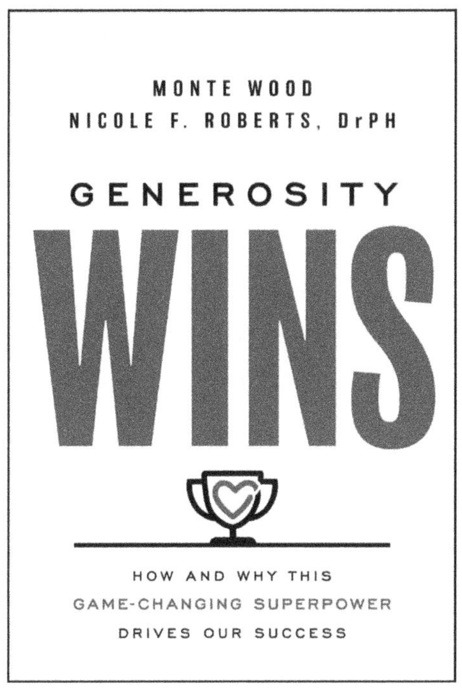

The authors came to me with a desire to do a book about generosity that would also incorporate interviews with 15 highly successful individuals whom the authors knew to be extraordinarily generous people. The question was, how do you turn a series of interviews with people into a book that others would want to read? I suggested they do a hybrid of fiction and non-fiction. Specifically, that we spin a tale around a young woman who worked for a top hotel chain whose mentor wanted her to learn the true meaning of generosity, so he put her in touch with these 15 individuals and had her fly from city to city to meet each of them in person and learn about generosity from them. In the story, she was on probation at work because her performance had faltered, and her mentor figure essentially said, "Either you go do these interviews, or you are going to lose your job."

Monte and Nicole ran with the idea. They did the interviews, and we turned those interviews into conversations between the fictional main character of the story and the real people, set in their offices and homes. The soufflé rose, and the book captures all the ideas about generosity the clients wanted to share with the readers. It is a really fun and engaging book and best of all, there is room for a sequel!

ZIG ZIGLAR

Born to Win: Find Your Success Code

I love Zig Ziglar. I will say it again in case I wasn't clear: I love Zig Ziglar. He is funny, down to earth, spiritual, smart, and above all, real. I got to hear him speak at events a few times after I had immersed myself in his books, audio, and videos. In his generation, he was the supreme motivator, sales trainer, and general "get the

best out of you" guy. So many of his ideas dictate the way I think and try to live. Zig was and is a profound influence on me, and I'm just one of tens of millions of people who feel that way.

"I wish I could sell you your brain for $100,000," Zig would say. "Because then you would appreciate your brain, and I would have $100,000!"

I was speaking with a publishing friend who told me that she was about to publish what would be Zig's last book. I told her I would edit it … for no fee. That is how much I loved Zig. This would be my opportunity to give back to him.

We did not meet face-to-face during the editing process. Instead, I wrote him a long letter based on the draft. I knew many of the stories he told in the book because I had heard them over and over again on audio or live. So I asked if he could finish the story and include points A, B, and C, the way he told it in one of his sales videos. Or I would suggest a story that might illustrate a point that he was making.

Imagine my rapture, if that is not too strong a term, when I found his acknowledgment in the book, "Thank you, Michael Levin, for making my best work even better."

That still gives me goosebumps to have been beneficial to an individual who benefitted so many.

It gets better. I became friends with his kids, Tom and Julie, who run the Ziglar consulting business, and they arranged for the four of us to have lunch. That is right—I got to have lunch with Zig Ziglar, Tom Ziglar, and Julie Ziglar-Norman in Plano, Texas. Does life get any better than that?

When I arrived, Zig looked at my jacket and tie—what else would I have worn?—and promptly commented, "You must be a married man. No single man could dress that nicely." And we were off and running.

It was a blast to sit there and talk with the man who had so deeply influenced my thinking about work, life, spirituality, and family relationships. I reminded him that I had even sent him a fan letter after he did a book on parenting when my youngest was two-years old. I even had her hold up on a copy of the book in a photo I took, and back then, you had to go to the drugstore to get prints made (man, I feel old saying that, and that was just 20 years ago!).

At the end of the lunch, just before we said goodbye, Zig told me, as only Zig could, "Be careful on the highway because accidents cause people."

Thank you, Zig, for making my best life even better.

DAVID B. PLOURDÉ, PH.D.

Solving the Weight Loss Puzzle: The Plourdé Method sm *Integrating Science, Psychology, and Faith in Your Weight Loss Solution*

These days, it is hard to find anyone who isn't trying or thinking about trying semaglutide, better known by its commercial name of Ozempic, for weight loss. Ozempic is a drug given to diabetics, and it has a positive side effect — it reduces the hunger people feel, so they eat less and lose a bunch of weight.

That is the positive side effect. Who am I to gainsay Big Pharma? Maybe there are no negative side effects. But maybe there will be. Time will tell. One thing's for sure – once you start it, if you stop taking it, you gain all the weight back. Oh, well.

In the meantime, Dr. David Plourdé has been helping people lose weight and specifically break through the weight loss plateau that so many of us, myself included, reach and simply cannot go beneath. I like to say that I have lost over a hundred pounds. The problem is that it is the same 20 pounds lost and regained over the last 20 years.

David has an unusual background for a diet doctor. He has a Ph.D. in human nutrition and exercise physiology, was a social work-er, and expected to go to seminary and follow a religious calling. In-stead, he has helped thousands of men and women lose weight, break through the weight loss barrier, and keep the weight off. The Plourdé Method, which he developed, controls the HSL enzyme, reducing cell and body fat levels in what he describes as an entirely predictable and reproducible fashion.

I don't know what that means exactly because I don't have a sci-ence background. I do know that David is the real deal.

We came together about five years ago to work on his book, but it turned out that the timing wasn't right, so he took time away from the project and picked it up again six months ago. And when he wrote it, he did it without any help from me.

I count him as one of my success stories, with his full permission, because he says that the ideas that I shared with him when we were working together stayed in his head for the five years between when we stopped working together and when he picked up the pen to get the project done.

Below are the key ideas that David credits for the book's completion, and he is kind enough to give me credit for them.

First, books are like babies — they have their own gestation periods, and they come when they think they should come, not when we think they should come. With books, as with everything else, timing is everything. You might think that this is the perfect time to do a book. The book might think otherwise! It does happen that projects aren't finished or are finished and aren't published simply because of timing.

This has nothing to do with the quality of the book, the quality of the writing, or the importance of the ideas. It is just that sometimes, books need a longer gestation period before the author has become entirely ready to put his ideas out into the world. So, the gestation period for David's book was longer, but when the time was right, he got it right out.

Next, be generous with your ideas. This sounds like a given, but many people, and David was initially in this group, are sometimes concerned about putting all their intellectual property, all their ideas, down on paper and out into the world. Some people are concerned that others might pick up their ideas and run with them. I always remind my clients that the more generous they are with information, the more readers will respond to that generosity. You are just putting good karma into the world, and there is seldom any downside.

Sometimes, people want to save certain ideas for a follow-up book. I always tell them to cram everything that they know into book one! That way, book one will be as robust as possible. And although clients may be concerned that they won't have enough to put into a second book, I tell them not to worry. People will come up to them and say, "I loved your book, but I don't understand why you didn't talk about such and such." This is where the author slaps her forehead and says to herself, "My gosh! How could I have forgotten to write about such and such?!" Or the proverbial light bulb goes off over the head of the author, and she says to herself, "Wow! What a great idea! I could do a whole book about that topic!"

In other words, you don't realize how much you know, not just about the specific topic you are writing about in book one, but how much *else* you know that can be topics for books two, three, four, and so on.

When you are writing a book, don't hold back. Put it all in. If it is too much, someone (probably me, for example) might tell you to dial it back a little. But usually, the more wisdom and guidance we provide, the more generous we are as authors, the better our books are, and the more they help people. David took that lesson to heart, and his book is a rich, complete, and thoroughly enjoyable read, one that is a force multiplier for his vital message about how to lose weight and keep it off successfully.

KEN DRUCK

How We Go On: Self-Compassion, Courage, and Gratitude on the Path Forward

I call Ken Druck the American Mother Teresa. He is the chief comforter and go-to person in moments of national or personal tragedy. After 9/11, Ken got the call to meet with the families of those who perished, including fallen firefighters and peace officers.

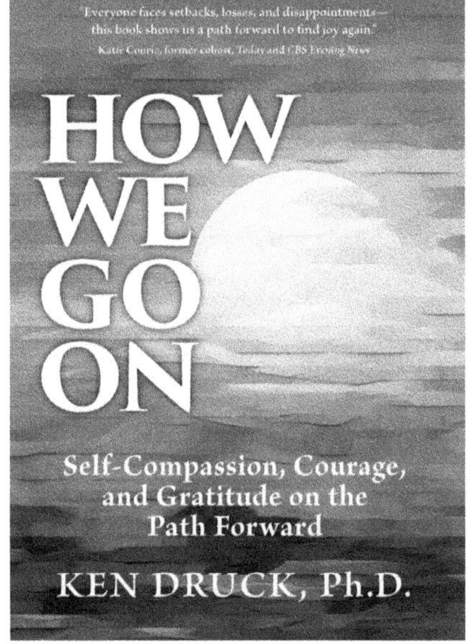

After Flight 800, Columbine, Sandy Hook, the Pittsburgh and San Diego synagogue shootings, and dozens of other mass tragedies, Ken was the guy brought in to help the survivors, responders, and communities summon the courage, faith, and strength to go on.

In his hometown of San Diego, Ken is the man who accompanies bereaved and traumatized families to the morgue to identify the bodies of their loved ones and begin their new lives. I shake my head as I write these words. How could any human being do any of this, let alone all of it?

Ken's capacity for processing traumatic loss was born when one of his daughters died while studying abroad. He honors his "angel daughter" by doing good in her name, helping families who have suffered comparable losses, and communing with her on his morning walks near the ocean.

I have edited many books for Ken over the last 20 years. These books offer readers the tools, techniques, tenacity, and self-compassion to find a way forward after life's turning points. Courageously growing, aging, adulting, parenting, surviving life's losses, and rising from adversity are all covered in Ken's life's work and books, some of which have become best sellers.

Ken channeled the love he has for his daughter, Jenna, into the Jenna Druck Center, which helped thousands of families find a path forward and showed thousands of teenage girls how to be leaders in their own lives and communities. Today, he channels the love of his surviving daughter, Stefie, and her twin sons in his life's work and life-affirming books. I call Ken the American Mother Teresa, and I will never understand the source of his courage and strength.

PETE LARRIEU

Pain Free Secrets: What "They" Don't Want You to Know

I fell out of love with organized medicine 20 years ago when I did a project for a gentleman on the Forbes List who owned a company that made medical devices. I had no problem with my client. I was shocked by what I learned when his COO toured me around the factory.

They made pacemaker batteries, among other things.

"Our batteries will last for 200 years," my host told me. "The FDA will only certify them for 25 years because nobody will believe that a battery would last two centuries. But they do. The problem is the heart surgeons. They won't use our batteries because they want people with pacemakers to come back every three years and have their battery replaced. If they used our batteries, they would lose a ton of business."

I'm from New York, so I'm not easily shocked, but this revelation took the air out of me. I'm sure there are heart surgeons who will use the 25-year battery. Otherwise, why would my client's company continue to manufacture them? The fact that an overwhelming number of heart surgeons won't use them and instead choose to put patients through the trauma and risk of an unnecessary surgery ... words fail me.

What I learned that day at my client's factory returned to my thoughts when I met Peter Larrieu, a rock drummer turned tennis champion turned body care specialist who calls himself Pain-Free Pete. I went to see him not because there was anything particularly wrong but because I had learned that he had a methodology for radically improving the flexibility of the human body. We ended up trading services—he has helped me stay fit, and I helped him with his book. And I will use an overused word, one that you won't find anywhere else in this volume, to describe Pain-Free Pete.

He is a genius.

I define genius as someone who sees things that others don't see and then creates a system for improving the lives of others based on the ideas they have developed. In Pete's case, the idea is simple yet profound. Why do people have so much pain in their bodies? Why do people require so much surgery on their joints, hips, elbows, and shoulders?

Here is Pete's answer: Those parts of the body are meant to carry weight - the weight of the human body itself and the weight of the things we lift and move. Unfortunately, the way we sit, hunched over our computers, the way we walk, bent over our phones, the way we drive, the way we play golf and tennis - all these activities have one thing in common. They cause the parts of the body to bear weight in ways that were never intended. The result is joint pain. The typical answer is physical therapy and then medication. And when that fails, surgery.

Pete found a better way:

Stretching.

Depending on the part of your body affected, Pete will put you through a series of stretches that you hold for anywhere from one to five minutes, as well as simple movements that you repeat 10 to 20 times. This immediately reduces the strain on your non-weight-bearing areas, and pain is typically relieved in that first session.

People go to Pete a few times to lock in precisely how to perform the stretches, and then they find that they don't have pain. They don't need physical therapy, drugs, or surgery, which, contrary to popular belief, often causes more problems than it solves.

That is the genius of Pain-Free Pete.

I run distance races—marathons, half-marathons, triathlons, trail runs, what have you. In the last 20 years, I have done more than 40 such races, including 10 Boston Marathons and eight New York City marathons. I am 65. I have no pain. Why? Because I do Pain-Free Pete's stretching program.

I have taken friends to see Pain-Free Pete. Some had been told they were unquestionable candidates for hip or knee replacements. In all cases, they came away from Pete's first session feeling better. Most of them didn't believe that a guy with a small stopwatch around his neck could possibly know more than the American medical establishment, so they went and had the surgery anyway, often with doleful results.

The first time I ran a half-marathon after I had been following Pete's protocol, I had the extraordinary experience of feeling as if I were running inside somebody else's body. I still feel that way today. If you have pain, you want this book. Or go to painfreepete.com and find the process relevant to your situation. Or better still, visit Pain-Free Pete in his facility in Irvine, California, and experience it for yourself.

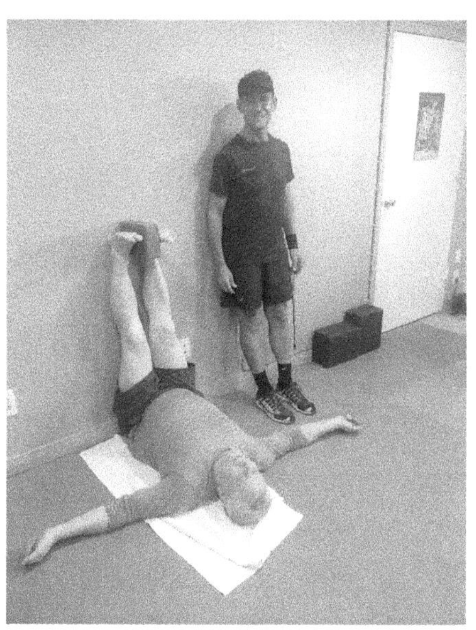

The author in a stretching session with Pain-Free Pete

SECTION 4
MEMOIRS

JOHN BRYANT

Banking on Our Future: A Program for Teaching You and Your Kids About Money

John Bryant grew up in Los Angeles and, like his fellow citizens, he was devastated by the civil unrest, or riots, or whatever you want to call them, that followed the Rodney King verdict in 1992. While there were always threats that the destruction would move from what was then called South Central Los Angeles to the three B's - Bel Air, Beverly Hills, and Brentwood, the tonier neighborhoods where white people lived - most of the destruction rained down upon the Black community in South Central where John had been raised.

By then, John had become a successful banker, and when he visited South Central after the devastation ended, he came to a powerful realization. The only stores and houses that burned down were those that were rented. *People don't burn what they own*, John realized.

John also knew that the difference between a monthly rental payment and a mortgage payment was minimal for most of the housing units in underprivileged communities like South Central, which is now called South Los Angeles. He realized that if he could create a program to clean up the credit records of South Central residents and somehow get banks to reduce or forego the need for a down payment, more and more people could become homeowners. This would add stability, safety, and continuity to neighborhoods ... because people don't burn what they own.

John took two actions that changed the course of Los Angeles and then other urban areas around the country. He created a nonprofit called Banking on Our Future, which served the precise purpose I outlined a moment ago. Let's clean up the credit ratings of renters so they can qualify to become home buyers. That way, we can improve neighborhoods like South Central one home at a time.

John also realized that he had to change the thinking of the LA banking community, which had always viewed South Central as a drug-infested war zone, more so after the civil unrest/riots (pick one) of Spring 1992. So, John famously organized "banker bus tours," where he loaded up loan officers from the city's major banks and took them on a field trip to South Central! To their shock and amazement, the bankers discovered that these were perfectly normal neighborhoods, perhaps with smaller houses than the neighborhoods where they lived, but the communities were entirely peaceful. You didn't see drug dealers with submachine guns on every corner. Yes, you saw more bars on the windows of the houses than you would see in the three B's: Beverly Hills, Bel Air, and Brentwood, but on the whole, South Central was a perfectly normal, livable, and by and large safe place to live … and more importantly, from the bankers' perspective, to make home loans.

John brought prospective home buyers to the banks and prospective bankers to South Central. It was a match made in heaven, and thousands upon thousands of individuals now own their homes in communities like South Central across the United States.

It just shows the power of an individual with insights that nobody else has combined with the power of hard work to turn those insights into success.

LARRY FIELD

Not So Bad - From the Bronx to Beverly Hills

Larry Field was born in the Bronx to parents who were Hungarian-Jewish immigrants and who ran a grocery store smaller than your living room. Larry went to work in his father's store while still in high school, working behind the counter, making deliveries, stocking the shelves, and doing whatever needed to be done. Larry's father was gregarious and encouraging and would frequently say in the boy's presence, "Everybody loves Larry!" Larry would just beam.

Larry studied business at Baruch College, part of the City University of New York, whose business school is now named for him. His first job was a sales position for Lever Brothers, where he sold more soap and a more expensive kind of soap than anyone in the company. Realizing that his career path was thwarted because of the anti-Semitism that ruled the corporate world at the time, Larry left Lever Brothers and then took a job in real estate, where he learned the ins and outs of the business.

His first major opportunity came in 1963 when New York was gearing up for the World's Fair. Larry realized that folks around the world would need housing adjacent to the fairgrounds in Queens, New York. He went to apartment owners, pitched himself as the middleman between the foreign visitors and the apartment owners, and ensured that there were hundreds of apartments under lease for the visiting Japanese Pavilion team members and others from around the world.

Larry parlayed his real estate knowledge and success into his own company, which he called NSB, Inc., which stood for the answer he would always give you if you asked him how he was: "Not so bad!" Larry went on to become one of the leading commercial real estate developers in Southern California, and when he passed at age 89, his obituary appeared in the Wall Street Journal.

Larry became a mentor whose business lessons shared in our interview sessions became guideposts in my career. My favorite story out of many is the time that Larry and his partner traveled to Calabasas, about an hour's drive from Los Angeles, to meet with an individual who had adamantly refused up until then to sell a property that Larry found extremely desirable.

They got to his office, cooled their heels in the waiting room for a long time, and were finally admitted into the owner's presence with the greeting that he had less than an hour before he had to catch a flight.

Larry took one look at the man, and his first question, "How much did you pay for your hair plugs?" nearly sent his partner into a state of shock.

"You write down how much you paid for your hair plugs," Larry told the seller, and remember, these were the first words he said to him, "and I'll write down how much I paid for mine. Whoever paid less has to give the other guy $100. Deal?"

The seller, amused, agreed. They both wrote down how much they had paid for each hair plug. Larry had paid a lower amount, so the seller took a 100-dollar bill out of his wallet and handed it to Larry, who pocketed it.

For the next 45 minutes, the two men spoke of nothing but hair plugs. Larry's shocked partner sat in the corner, turning colors.

Finally, the seller looked at his watch.

"I've got to catch a flight," he said. "I'll sell you the property. Let's make a deal." And they did.

They always tell you to keep the initial part of the conversation, the rapport-building phase, short and sweet in sales classes. Larry had no use for rules like that. He did things his way. And he always got the deal.

Including that time after the extremely extended discussion about hair plugs.

Once, I asked Larry if he had any regrets in business.

"Yes," he said. "I regret that I didn't buy every single-family home in Beverly Hills in 1973."

Oh, well. Everybody loves Larry.

JOAQUIN "JACK" GARCIA

Making Jack Falcone: An Undercover FBI Agent Takes Down a Mafia Family

Sometimes, clients ask me which book, out of all the books I've done, is my favorite. If I'm being smart, I tell them it is their book. If I'm being honest, I tell them it is *Making Jack Falcone*. Jack Garcia is a Cuban émigré, and we bonded in our first call over the fact that my mother and her family spent World War II in Havana, having escaped

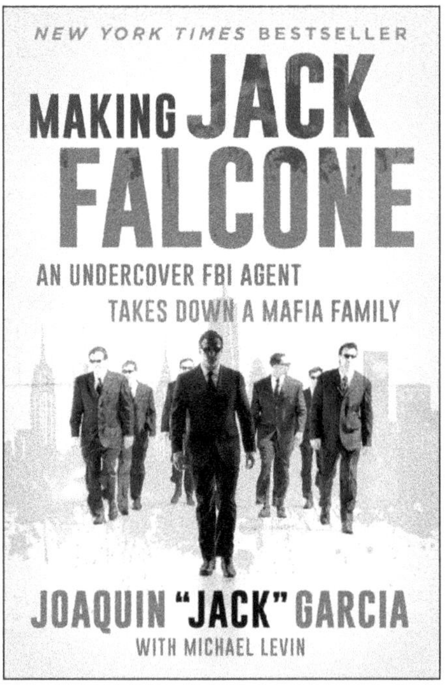

the Nazi Holocaust. Our Havana connection became the foundation of a great working relationship and, as often happens with my clients, an enduring friendship.

Jack, like many immigrants, including myself, fell in love with the freedom and opportunity that the United States offered, in contrast with the stark limits communist Cuba imposed on its citizens. Jack saw a movie called *Serpico* when he was a teen, and he was so inspired by that film that he decided he would go into law enforcement when he got older. Coincidentally, I read *Serpico* when I was a teen, and that is when I decided I was going to become a writer.

Jack kept his word and became an FBI agent. Not only that, but he became the most accomplished and decorated undercover agent in the history of the Bureau. Donnie Brasco might have had more fame, but Jack scoffed at "Brasco" on the grounds that his cases were so much smaller than the ones Jack tackled.

A literary agent introduced Jack and me, convinced there was a book about Jack's work as an undercover agent inside the Gambino crime family of the New York Mafia. Jack had embedded himself inside a Westchester County crime crew for more than two years, convincing them he was Jack Falcone, a jewel thief from Florida, rather than Jack Garcia, an FBI agent from Havana. Jack traveled with his crew, his cover only an issue when he was ordered to beat people who hadn't paid up on time. Somehow, Jack always found a way to use his sheer size - he was 6'4" and 390 pounds in those days - to intimidate without laying hands on the slow payers.

While operating undercover with the Gambinos, Jack was simultaneously handling three other major undercover cases. One involved imported supernotes; fake, precisely made $100 bills imported from North Korea. A second was a major terrorism case in the New York area. The third case involved illegal gambling operations. So, the challenge of writing his book was simply organizing the material without bewildering the reader. Jack's daughter, then 10, was bewildered about her father's real identity. He had four first names, four cell phones, and four cars he would drive home in, depending on which identity he would inhabit the next day. Occasionally, Jack would tell me, "No interviews next week. I'm going undercover in Florida." This would get me thinking please don't get killed while you are down there!

The finishing touch was when the manuscript was complete, and I received a call from someone who claimed to be the nephew of the main Mafioso detailed in the book. He asked if he could come down to my office and read the galleys. Panicked, I called Jack.

"What does the Mafia do to coauthors?" I asked, scared out of my wits.

"Ha!" Jack exclaimed. "Two to the back of the head!"

The guy didn't come down. Mercifully, I never heard from him again. Instead, the book became a New York Times best seller and was promptly optioned by Paramount and the great director Steven Soderbergh. Working with Jack was a thrill ride, and fortunately, both he and I lived to tell the tale.

MYRON SUGERMAN

The Chronicles of the Last Jewish Gangster: From Meyer to Myron

Myron Sugarman would be a little more than a footnote to history, an individual who spent more than 60 years in the fields of casinos and illegal gambling around the world, were it not for one thing. He is the last surviving link to an era of Jewish gangsters in New Jersey, stemming from the 1930s to the 1950s.

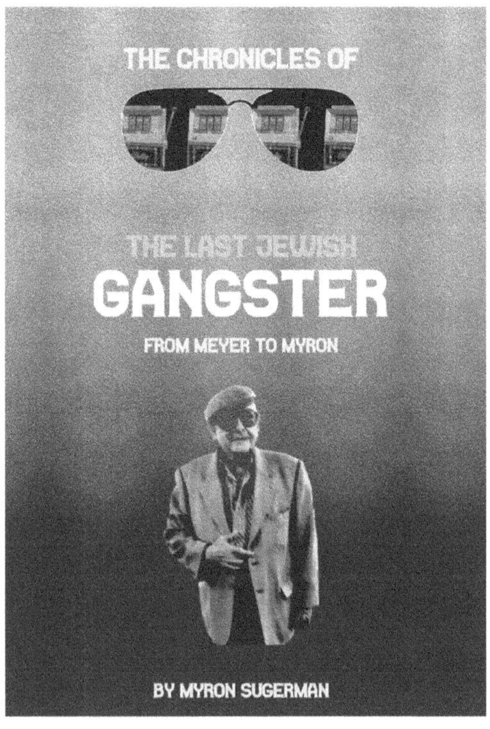

Myron says that Jews formed Mafia-like gangs for the same reason immigrant Italians did - they could not get justice in the American justice system, so they had to find their own ways to protect themselves. Myron's father was also a small-time gangster, but he worked with and introduced his son to some of the biggest names in crime, including Meyer Lansky, Longi Zwillman, and Gerry Catena, a leading member of the Genovese crime family in New York. Myron told me about the pro-Nazi groups that would march in World War II-era Newark and other cities and towns in New Jersey. The Jewish mobs were the only entities that would provide any protection from those groups for the immigrant Jews living in those places.

Those experiences sent Myron off on a career of what he describes as "disorganized crime," which would find him installing casino equipment in cities and towns from Africa to South America. For the most part, law enforcement left him unmolested, and on the rare occasions he was shot at. Fortunately, they missed. Myron ended up doing some prison time but emerged none the worse for wear. He lectures on the book throughout the Tristate area and in Florida, the last link to a lost world.

BUD KERENTOFF

*Building Blocks to a
Wonderful Life*

Bud Karentoff was never famous. A farmer and small businessman, his most public position had been on the city council in his small town in Michigan decades earlier. Sandi Karentoff, his daughter, who had commissioned the book, came to me because she wanted me to capture her father's story. When I interviewed Bud, he was 95. Bud

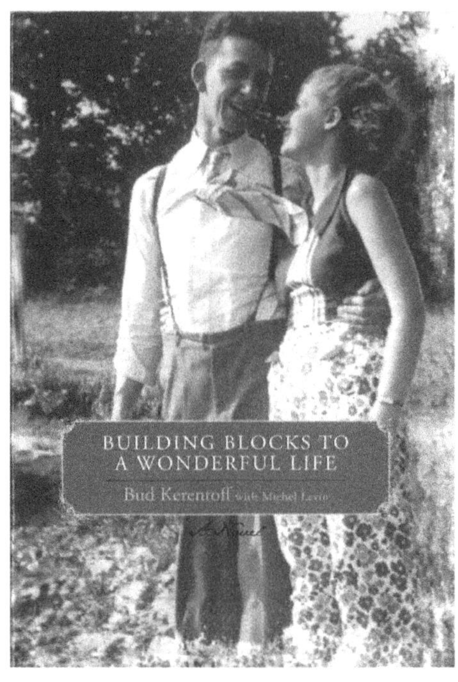

saw cars come in, and then he saw the internet come in. That is a pretty long lifespan! He told me about the Roaring 20s, the Depression, World War II, and the good times in the "American Century" that followed. My favorite recollection of Bud's has to do with his stories about sex, or the lack thereof, among teenagers in the 1910s, when he was coming of age. He told me, point blank, that most people his age, 16 or 17, had simply never heard of sex. The question of where babies came from was immaterial, and the question of what married people did behind closed doors was of absolutely no interest. I still find it incredibly entertaining that a generation of young people could grow up without the slightest idea that sex even existed. It was probably a lot easier to be a parent back then!

When I contacted Sandi to ask if I could write about her father's book for this project, she wrote back and said, "Absolutely! It is the best decision I ever made!"

For somebody who does what I do, it doesn't get any better than that.

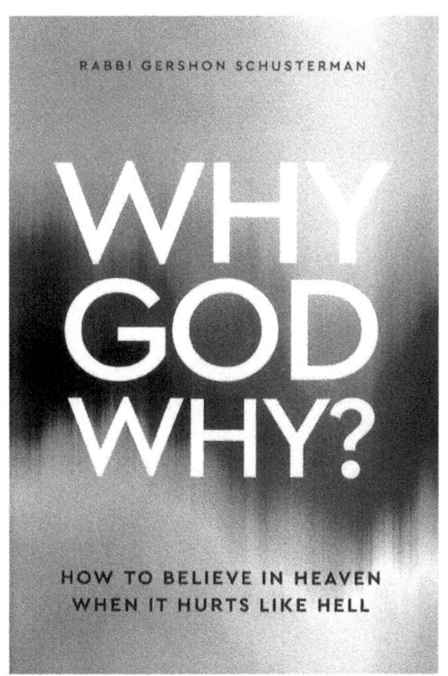

RABBI GERSHON SCHUSTERMAN

Why God Why? How to Believe in Heaven when it Hurts Like Hell

Rabbi Gershon Schusterman was married with ten children, ran a religious day school in Southern California, and counseled community members, school parents, and others on life and death matters, as do most religious leaders. And then tragedy struck Gershon: his wife died suddenly in her late 30s, leaving the Rabbi with ten children to raise and a lot of questions to answer.

The primary question Rabbi Schusterman had to answer for himself was whether the answers he had been giving to grieving congregants and others he counseled had any validity. It's another thing to go through it yourself, having to explain the loss of your beloved wife not just to yourself but to your children and the entire faith-based community.

In his book Why God Why? Rabbi Schusterman offers the conclusions he reached based on his own experience and his deep knowledge of Judaism. The book tackles the hardest questions: what is evil, and why does it exist? Is there really a God? Is it okay to be angry with God? Is suffering a test of faith? How do we understand the Holocaust? What does Judaism have to say about the afterlife? And if there is no explanation for loss, how do we reach a place of peace?

It's always dicey to describe a book as an "instant classic," but the term certainly applies to Rabbi Schusterman's book, which sold thousands upon thousands of copies in the first two years of publication.

Rabbi Schusterman reports an enormous sense of satisfaction at being able to share his hard-won lessons, created in the crucible of his own inexplicable loss, with so many.

ABRAHAM ZUCKERMAN

A Voice in the Chorus: Life as a Teenager in the Holocaust

In 1986, I attended the Bar Mitzvah given by my cousin Abraham Zuckerman for his grandson. You think you haven't heard of Abe, but if you saw *Schindler's List*, you saw him. He and his two partners went through the concentration camps and owed their lives to Schindler, who would do things

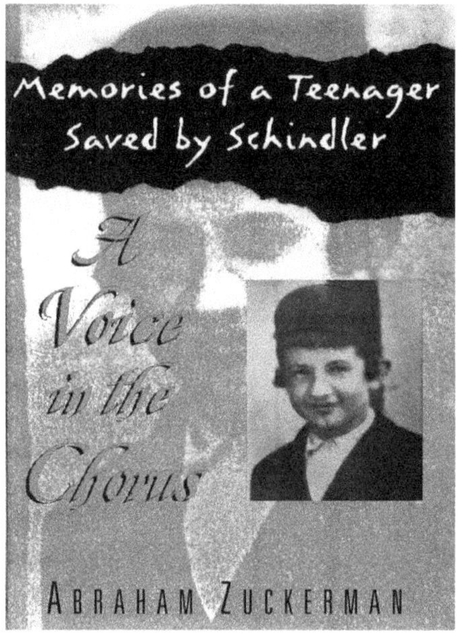

like leave extra potatoes out for the prisoners so they wouldn't starve to death or treat his Nazi overseers at his factory to booze and prostitutes so they wouldn't look too closely at the operation he was running, which was primarily about saving Jews.

Abe survived the camps and then spent four years at a displaced persons camp at a place called Bindermichel, Austria, where he met and fell in love with the woman he married, my Aunt Millie. Part of the attraction about Millie was that she had survived with her entire family, which was practically unique. Most of the young men like Abe at the displaced person's camp had lost their parents and siblings, and they were the sole survivors in their families. Not so for Millie, who survived with her parents and sister because a righteous Polish gentile woman hid the lot of them in her attic for two years, Anne Frank-style, where they sat for all that time without saying a word. If you can imagine such a thing.

Abe and Millie meet and get married, and Abe comes to the United States, where he starts building and selling houses before he really learns English. Abe was extremely handy, which actually saved his life as a teenager in the camps. When anyone was sent to a new camp, they would line all the new inmates up at the Appellplatz, the central meeting place, and ask if anybody had skills. Abe was very handy, and he would always say he was an electrician. He was 15, by the way. A 15-year-old electrician saving his own life because he could do things like string lights across a quarry, or when he was 16 and in another camp after Schindler's, working in a factory built into a hillside so it could not be bombed, building Messerschmidt jet aircraft.

So here's Abe, 20 years old, married, now living in New Jersey as a refugee, speaking virtually no English, and somehow, he's building houses. Go figure. Abe goes on to build so many houses with his two partners and make so much money that when they find Oskar Schindler destitute, like most of the rest of Germany after the war, he and his partners pay for the rest of Schindler's life as a way of expressing gratitude for the fact that he saved theirs.

So here we are at the Bar Mitzvah for Abe's grandson, who has known nothing but the finer things in life, having grown up in great wealth as part of Abe's extended family. Did his grandfather ever take him to visit one of the dozens of Schindler Streets, Schindler Avenues, or Schindler Places that Abe created in the dozens of communities he developed throughout New Jersey and Pennsylvania? I don't know. I do know that when Abe got up to speak, he was in tears, and before long, so were the rest of us.

"When I was 15 in the camps," he began, "stringing electric lights over quarries, I never imagined in a million years I would have a future.

I never imagined I would live to become an adult, or get married, or have a family, or succeed. None of that seemed remotely possible.

"And yet, here we are, celebrating the Bar Mitzvah of my grandson. For someone like me, who grew up in Poland, whose father made a living sewing shtreimelach, fur hats for Shabbos and the Jewish holidays, at his kitchen table, to be living here in America … all of it seems incredible."

Those weren't his exact words, but they were close enough, and the whole room was convulsed with tears, except for the Bar Mitzvah boy and his friends, who were 13 and couldn't have cared less. When Abe came off the stage, he glanced at them, and you could see the frustration that they weren't paying attention to one of the most important moments of his life etched into his features. He glanced meaningfully at me, and his look said very simply, "We are going to write a book," and we did.

Writing Abe's book took four years. Every few months, we would meet at the piano bar at the Hilton at 6th Avenue and 45th Street in Manhattan, and he would give me the broad facts surrounding his experiences growing up in Krakow, Poland, then one of the great seats of Eastern European Jewry, the onset of the war, forced labor, and then separation from his family and incarceration in the concentration camps. And then Bindermichel, and then meeting his wife, and then coming to America. I would go home, take that information, and turn it into a long series of questions. My feeling was that the sheer numbers of the Holocaust made it impossible for the human mind to grasp. So, instead of focusing on statistics, I wanted specifics. How was he transported from one camp to another? What did he wear? What did he eat? What was a day like? What was his attitude and the attitude of the other prisoners? Remember that Abe was 12 when he went into the camps and 16 when the war ended. And now he was in his 60s, looking back. I wanted him to dredge up with specificity every memory that he could, even the ones he had suppressed so that together, we could create a book that would bring the reality and the horror of the Holocaust home.

And that's what we did. He would take those questions and answer them on a tape recorder, his assistant would type them out and send them to me, and I would turn them into drafts of chapters. We would review them at the piano bar at the Hilton, and he would add in fresh details, memories that he didn't even know he had forgotten, to make the chapters even more robust, more real, and more impossible to ignore. He used to marvel at the swirl of tourists and businesspeople surrounding us at the piano bar. If only they knew what we were doing, they would be astonished. Nobody stopped to ask. Nobody bothered us.

And four years after we started, Abe's book, *A Voice in the Chorus*, was finished. Since Abe was one of the founders of the Holocaust Museum in Washington DC, his book was on sale there. Abe went from high school to high school throughout New Jersey and beyond, giving away copies of the books, telling his story to astonished schoolchildren, and always reminding them, "Never forget!" I think of the Jews of Abe's era, the survivors, the escapees, and those who were lost, as the Jewish 'Greatest Generation.' We have no idea what they went through, and we will never have a clear idea of what they went through, but by writing Abe's book and later Millie's memoirs, too, I had a taste of that experience.

At one point, I started having nightmares about the Holocaust, and I described those nightmares to Abe. "Those are the nightmares we have," he said, and I felt that, in a small way, I was part of that fraternity, one of them.

HUGH O'BRIAN WITH VIRGINIA O'BRIAN

Hugh O'Brian, or What's Left of Him

If you are old enough to re-member, Hugh O'Brian was one of the most famous and handsome movie and TV stars of his era. You, or perhaps more likely your parents or your grandparents, would remember him from *The Life and Legend of Wyatt Earp*, an ABC series that ran from 1955 to 1961. Hugh was so famous that when the

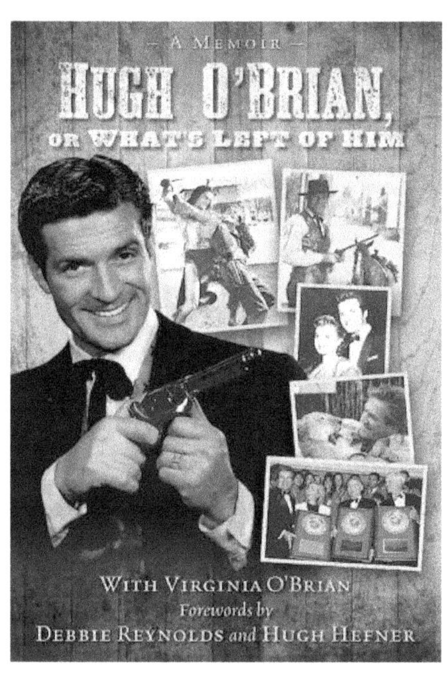

Beatles came to Los Angeles in 1965, they visited him.

Hugh wanted a memoir to capture not just his career but also his devotion to the Marines and to the Hugh O'Brian Youth Leadership Foundation, a nonprofit youth leadership - development program for high school students. More than half a million students have gone through the program since he founded it in 1958. Hugh told me that he had the idea for the program after visiting Albert Schweitzer, the Nobel Peace Prize-winning minister and physician who created and ran a hospital in French Equatorial Africa, now Gabon. Hugh visit-ed Schweitzer at his hospital and came away asking himself what he could do for others, and the HOBY Foundation was born.

If you called Hugh and you got his answering tape, he would tell you, "You've got Hugh O'Brian, or what is left of him." Hence the book title.

To put it mildly, Hugh had never met a woman he could not charm. So I will never forget the time that he met my assistant, a young woman who had a religious practice of not shaking hands with men. Hugh, then in his 80s, was perplexed. Had he lost his charm? Was he no longer the sex symbol he had been decades earlier?

When the religious issue was explained, he nodded, and then he was prepared for her next visit. He had a huge fake hand with him, and he made her shake hands with the fake hand. His record of never failing to charm a woman remained intact.

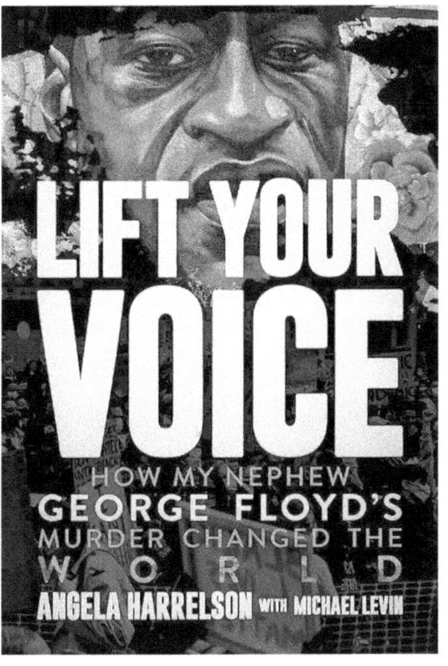

ANGELA HARRELSON

Lift Your Voice: How My Nephew George Floyd's Murder Changed the World

Angela Harrelson works as a nurse in a Minneapolis hospital. On May 25, 2020, she found that her phone was blowing up with messages from friends and family members telling her to find a video that had gone viral. The video depicted the shocking killing of her nephew, George Floyd, when Derek Chauvin, a Minneapolis police officer, famously kept his knee on Floyd's neck, making it impossible for him to breathe. The entire world watched the video with horror, but no one could have been as deeply affected as Angela, George's aunt and his closest relative in Minneapolis. A few months after the murder, I got a message from my assistant. "You have an Angela Harrelson on your calendar this morning," it said. "That is the same name as George Floyd's aunt."

Sure enough, it was she. We talked, and she told me that although a lot of people were coming to her trying to convince her to do a book, she didn't want to do something simply for the money. She looked at my website and, for whatever reason, decided I was the one.

The family didn't call him George. He went by the name Perry, and he had grown up in a dangerous, drug-infested neighborhood in Houston. Perry's legal troubles are well-known; he served four years in prison for his drug-related crimes. What most people don't know, and what Angela explains, is that Perry had moved to Minneapolis to get clean and sober. He had gone into a Salvation Army live-in recovery program, was working two jobs, and had more than a year of clean time when his mother's health declined precipitously. Perry wanted to go down to Houston to visit her and say goodbye, but his mother told him not to come. She said he was doing so well in Minneapolis and that if he came back to the Fourth Ward neighborhood in Houston where they lived, his sobriety would be at risk. So Perry stayed in Minneapolis and was devastated when his mother passed away without his having been able to say goodbye face-to-face.

Angela says that at this point, Perry left his Salvation Army program, his two jobs, and his sobriety behind. He went back to street crime and was trying to pass a counterfeit $20 bill when Chauvin took his life. Americans, sitting at home with nothing to do during the COVID shutdowns, watched that video over and over. Millions took to the streets around the world. Angela wrote her book so the world would know the real Perry, not the one who had been short-handed as a typical Black hoodlum. She also wanted to present her beliefs about how America's fractured race relations could be mended. Angela's dream was that whites could learn to acknowledge and, to some degree, renounce their entitlement while Blacks could learn to forgive. What a privilege to help carry that message.

CLAIRE WINELAND AND CHYNNA BRACHA LEVIN

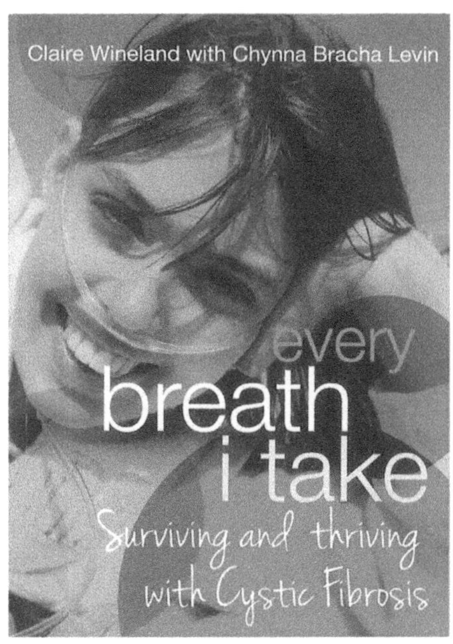

*Every Breath I Take:
Surviving and Thriving
with Cystic Fibrosis*

Claire Wineland, the daughter of a dear friend, was born with cystic fibrosis, a genetic disorder that primarily affects the lungs and digestive system, where the lungs are continually filled with mucus, making it increasingly difficult to breathe. Until only recently, the prognosis for people with CF was that they would barely make it out of their teens. Claire's family was committed to the idea that she would beat the odds.

One of my clients, a college friend who had become a highly successful businessman in Manhattan, had told me that one of his sons had written a book as a bar mitzvah project. My daughter was nearing bat mitzvah age, and she needed a project. Why not have her interview Claire and the two girls could do the book together, I thought?

Everyone was on board with the idea, and my daughter, Chynna, then 11, conducted phone interviews with Claire, then 13, over a period of months, and the book was published in time for Chynna's bat mitzvah. Claire attended and spoke, and the two girls, Claire wheeling her oxygen tank, moved from table to table, jointly signed copies of the book for each guest.

Claire subsequently became an internet sensation, an influencer, and a spokesperson for thriving with life-threatening illness. She survived several close calls and ultimately succumbed at age 21. Her Wikipedia entry describes her as "An American activist, author, speaker, and social media personality." All true.

The book was an Amazon best seller for more than seven years after its publication in 2012.

LOWELL KLESSIG AND LUKAS KLESSIG

Words With My Father—A Bipolar Journey Through Turbulent Times

Lukas Klessig's father, Lowell, was a journalist, an environmental activist, and a leader in his Midwestern farming community. He suffered from bipolar disorder, and when feelings overwhelmed him, he would retreat to his study and write thousands upon thousands of words. When he passed, his literary output, carefully arranged and cataloged, ranged hundreds of thousands of words.

Lukas wanted to create a fitting monument to his father, while at the same time processing his feelings about the highly complex individual who had raised him. How to do all that in one book?

I started to think about the song *Unforgettable*, a Nat King Cole hit in the 1960s. Several decades later, recording technology had advanced to the point where his daughter, Natalie Cole, a great singer in her own right, was able to record vocals that could be added to her father's original version of the song so that you now had a duet. And *Unforgettable*, this time, with father and daughter, topped the charts once again.

Why not do the same thing with the work of the Klessig père et fils? I suggested to Lukas that we take the parts of his father's memoir and some of his father's essays that were the most descriptive of his father's life and the most emblematic of his own writing and then have Lukas provide a commentary on each of those pieces of writing. So the book would be a conversation, if you will, between father and son, with the father describing his own life and the son describing his feelings about and reaction toward what his father had written.

The soufflé rose, and the result was *Words With My Father,* a poignant tribute to a father's memory on the part of a son who loved his father and wanted more than anything else to understand what drove him. The book intersperses Lowell's memoirs with Lukas's reflections on the events his father discusses. Lukas was happy, and so are his and his father's readers.

CAREY NEESLEY

Welcome Home Mama and Boris: How a Sister's Love Saved a Fallen Soldier

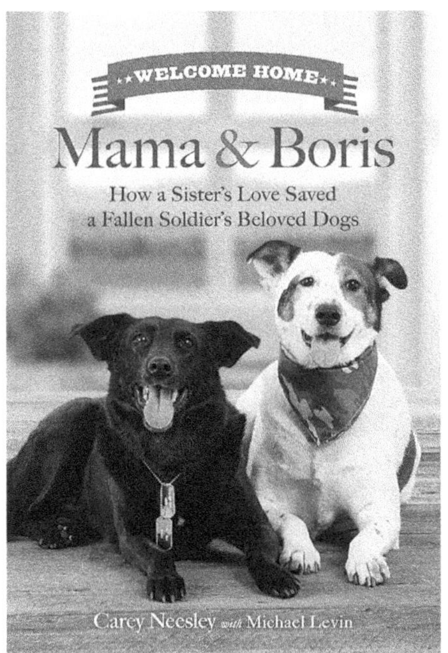

Let's get one thing straight - you are not allowed to have pets on a military base in a war zone. Are we clear? Carey Neesley's brother, serving in Baghdad during the Second Gulf War, didn't have much use for that particular regulation, and it turned out that many of his fellow servicemen and women ignored the rule, too. Tragically, Peter Neesley was killed in action on Christmas Day, 2007. Carey, who had an incredibly close relationship with her brother, was overwhelmed by the idea of planning his funeral. So instead, she turned her attention to his two dogs, who were living inside the wire on the base in Baghdad, without a caregiver.

At considerable personal risk, Carey flew into Baghdad while the war was still going on and somehow got the dogs home. When word of her feat became public, Carey started getting calls from family members of other fallen servicemen and women whose pets were still in war zones. Carey flew not once but multiple times into Afghanistan … and brought the dogs home.

She continues to work with organizations dedicated to bringing home wartime strays.

JULIETTA KHANTEYA THONG

Khanteya: My Courageous Quest for Love and Freedom

The Cambodian Holocaust began when Julie Thong was in her late teens. She believed with good reason that she and her family would be murdered if they stayed put. So she led her parents on a trek through the jungle, displaying incredible personal courage for a 17-year-old girl and eventually finding freedom and safety in neighboring Thailand at a Red Cross refugee camp.

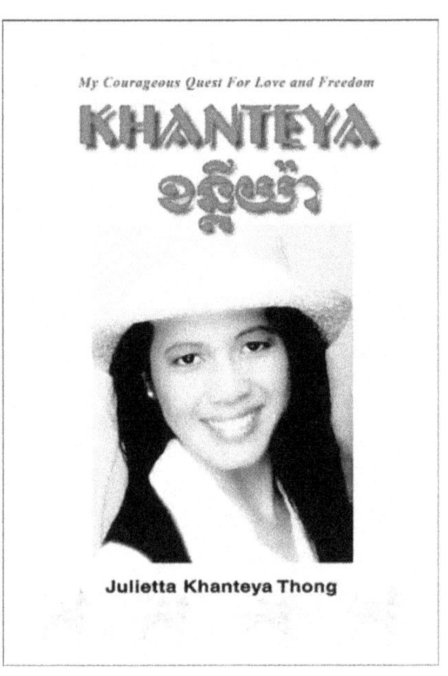

Julietta Khanteya Thong

Julie found more than freedom. She and a Swiss Red Cross doctor ten years older than she fell in love. She didn't feel that she could leave her family and stay with him, however, so they separated for some years, and then finally made plans to reunite in his native Switzerland. By the time Julie arrived in Switzerland, sadly, the doctor, not out of his 30s, had passed away from a previously undetected genetic condition.

Subsequently, Julie established herself in the thriving Cambodian community in Long Beach, California. Coming to this country with literally nothing, she ended up, within 15 years, a newly minted millionaire through her work in the cosmetic industry. Julie wanted to tell her story to demonstrate several key points. First, life takes courage, and sometimes, you have to rise to an occasion that you might not think you can handle. And second, when love becomes available, don't hesitate. Grab it.

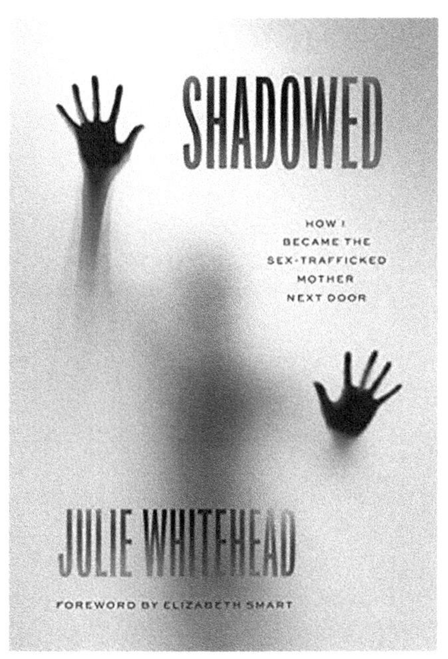

JULIE WHITEHEAD

Shadowed: How I Became the Sex-Trafficked Mother Next Door, with a foreword by Elizabeth Smart

Julie Whitehead never had it easy. Sexually abused by her father from early childhood, she went into a marriage with a sexually and physically abusive man in her late teens. Leaving such marriages is never easy, and this was compounded by the fact that her religious beliefs kept her from being comfortable with the idea of getting divorced.

A man stepped into her life who seemed like the perfect rescuer. He was the first person to whom Julie could confide about her sexual abuse in childhood and the bizarre nature of her marriage. Her husband would even insist that she fill out questionnaires he created if she wanted to have another child. She would speak about the agony of waiting for him to "grade" her questionnaire and give her an answer. The "savior" turned out to be anything but. Instead, he recruited an unwilling Julie into sex trafficking. Every weekend, this mother of three young children living in a small Utah community would be forced to prostitute herself in truck stops and other unsavory locations throughout the American West. It took more than a year before Julie could break free and five years of therapy before she was ready to tell her story. One hundred percent of the book's proceeds go to assisting survivors of sex trafficking and exploitation through the Malouf Foundation, which sponsored the creation of the book.

FANYA CARTER

All the Best: The Life of Victor M. Carter

Victor Carter came to the United States in the 1910s, like so many other immigrants from Russia, with little more than the proverbial clothes on his back. He ended up in Los Angeles, which was a tiny enclave, one that the nascent movie industry had just discovered because of its warm weather. Like the movie pioneers, Victor saw opportunity in the sunshine. He opened

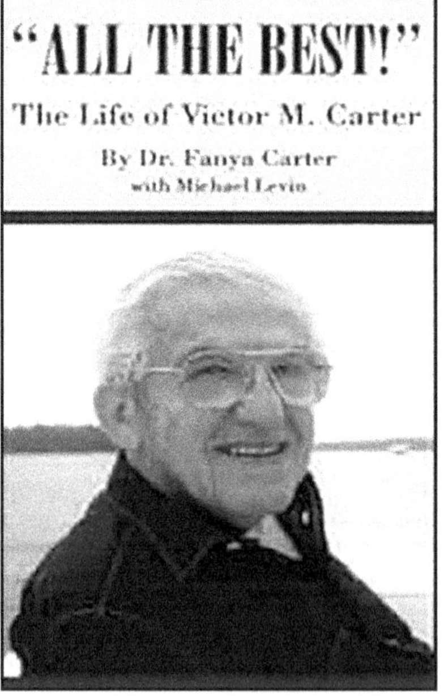

a small hardware store, which before long became a large hardware store, and which became, before much longer, a massive hardware store comprising an entire city block. Victor eventually sold the store and retired in his mid-30s, only to discover that retirement, after a few years of pleasant idleness, suited him poorly.

At about the same time, America was gearing up for its entry into World War II, which required a massive retooling of its industrial base. This was a topic Victor Carter knew something about, and he bought factories and created companies practically out of nothing that spun out huge amounts of material for the war effort. He became a "dollar a year man" - an industrialist tapped by the government for his brain power and given a token "salary" of one dollar per annum. Victor's contributions to the war effort won him considerable acclaim - and a second retirement.

After a few years, this new period of idleness suited him as poorly as had the first. So Victor, a longtime resident of Los Angeles and who had grown up with the city's movie industry, went into the entertainment business. He started his own studio and became as wildly successful in making motion pictures as he had been as a young hardware entrepreneur and a middle-aged war products industrialist.

In addition to his three careers, what really set Victor Carter apart was his incredible generosity and philanthropy. His daughter, Fanya Carter, a longtime therapist based in Santa Monica, took me to Victor's office and showed me the two huge index card containers that listed the hundreds and hundreds of charitable entities that Victor supported. Indeed, Victor Carter paid for the buses that took the Los Angeles contingent across the country to Martin Luther King, Jr.'s 1964 March on Washington. Victor Carter was with Dr. King the night before he delivered the "I Have a Dream" speech.

Fanya simply did not want her father's story to disappear, which is why we did the book.

SECTION 5
SPORTS

BENJAMIN WATSON

The New Dad's Playbook: Gearing up for the Biggest Game of Your Life

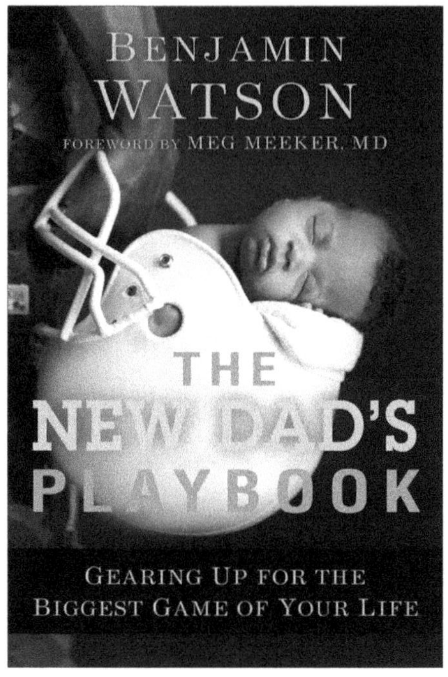

Benjamin Watson (his friends call him Benjamin, not Ben) is a Super Bowl-winning tight end with my beloved New England Patriots. He is also a devout Christian, and it bothered him enormously that a marker of "manhood" for athletes was to father multiple children with multiple women and then ignore their parental responsibilities. Benjamin, a devoted husband, and father of seven, wanted to take what he knew about parenting, specifically the question of how to support your wife as she goes through pregnancy and childbirth and share that guidance with fellow players and the world.

My wife was pregnant with our fourth child while I was working on the book, so it was a lot of fun for me to talk about parenting with Benjamin. The table of contents was also hugely enjoyable to assemble. The book is in five sections: Part one, training camp, which explains what the husband should expect when his wife becomes pregnant. Part two, the regular season, which covers her changing needs, baby showers, and budgeting. Part three, the Super Bowl, with two chapters: First, scrimmaging - last-minute preparations and, of course, game day, labor, delivery, and your first moments with your child. Part four, post-game, and Part five, off-season - the second child and beyond.

Football is a violent sport, but I've never met a more tender dad than Benjamin, and the book was a joy to produce. Remarkably, seven years after its publication, the book is still an Amazon best seller, with only a couple of dozen books ahead of Benjamin's. And a bunch of those are actually compilations of dad jokes.

Benjamin always spoke of his responsibility as a father to prepare children to be presented to God when they turn 18. I have no doubt that all seven of his kids will make the grade.

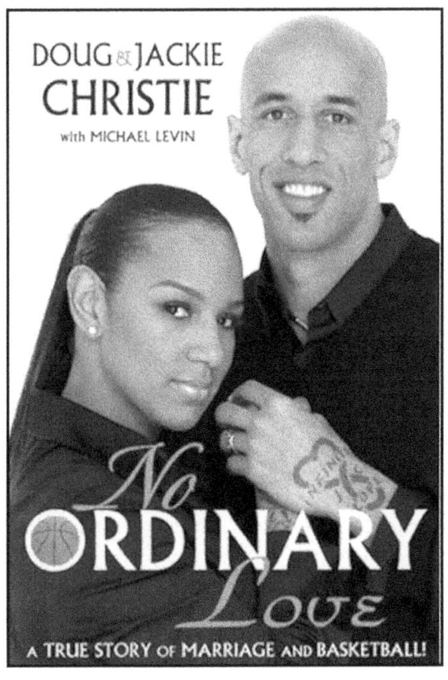

DOUG AND JACKIE CHRISTIE

No Ordinary Love: A True Story Of Love And Basketball!

If you're an NBA fan, then the name Doug Christie probably has some resonance for you. He was a star with the great Sacramento Kings teams of the 1990s, and he played equally well for a handful of other NBA squads. But Doug is remembered not just for his basketball skills but also for another trait—he was faithful to his wife.

Doug didn't fit the "bad boy" image of the NBA, an image that the Association has always worked hard to cultivate in its marketing campaigns. Bad boys have girlfriends. Lots of them. Not Doug. He and his wife Jackie both grew up in straightened circumstances in Seattle, and they both wanted a stable marriage based on faithfulness and spirituality. In the NBA, that's just plain wacky.

Doug was famous for having exactly one phone number on his cell phone—his wife's. Unlike many of his fellow NBA players, married or otherwise, Doug did not pursue other women. This made him a challenge to some of the women who worked in the front office in city after city where he played. Most people don't know the full story behind Doug's career. It happened repeatedly that Doug would be traded to a team, and a member of the front office staff would say, "I'm going to be the one who has a relationship with Doug. I'm going to take him down." And the pursuit was on. When they discovered that Doug's commitment to fidelity in his marriage was true and that he had no interest in dating or sleeping with women who worked for his employer, or any women, for that matter, they filed grievances against him, claiming sexual harassment.

It sounds upside-down and through the looking glass, but that's exactly what happened. Doug, whom I can tell you from firsthand experience is one of the most courteous and humble individuals I have ever met, was dogged in his career by a reputation for causing trouble when nothing could have been further from the truth.

Doug told me that he retired from the NBA not because he wanted to or because his skills had diminished but because his reputation for troublemaking around women, which is so bizarre when you consider the fact that he has always been faithful to his wife, preceded him. He had gotten to try out for Mike Dunleavy, then the head coach for the Clippers, and that would have been his final NBA team. The trial could not have gone better. And then Dunleavy checked in with colleagues and heard the rumors about Doug, the false rumors, I should add. Doug was not invited to join the team.

The matter might have ended there after he left the NBA, but Doug and Jackie had a dream. They wanted to create high-quality, low-income housing in their native Seattle. The problem was that their reputation—that same false and even libelous reputation that had followed Doug in his NBA career—followed them to Seattle. The business community was having a hard time taking the Christies seriously as legitimate partners in real estate development. The Christies had become sick and tired of the lies and simply refused to be denied the opportunity to create better housing opportunities in the communities where they had grown up. So, they reached out to me, introduced by a mutual friend who vouched for the quality of my work.

They explained the situation and said there was an opportunity to go into a real estate deal, but the deadline was just five weeks away. They wanted a hardcover book written about Doug's career and their relationship to set the record straight and counter all the lies that had been told about them in the media. For all those qualities as a stand-out player and faithful husband, the media portrayed Doug as some kind of nut. Why? Because he didn't fit the narrative of the NBA player as sexual predator. And if you don't think that's the narrative, take a look at the way the NBA markets its stars. Could we get the book in five weeks from interviews to publication? That was a pretty cool challenge, I thought. Let's get it done.

I interviewed the Christies for twelve hours over the course of a day and a half at the Ritz Carlton at Marina del Ray in California. As I've described elsewhere in these pages, an hour of interview leads to one chapter of book, and so it went with the Christies. I created an outline, and we stuck to it, completing the next chapter every hour. After a day and a half of interviews, the interview phase was complete. I rushed the audio of the conversations to my transcriptionist, who had them back the next day. I drafted each chapter in one to two hours. I didn't sleep a lot that week. I remember my oldest daughter, then five years old, lying next to me in bed while I feverishly composed the chapters. You can say the quality of my parenting slid a little that week, but she thought it was pretty cool that her daddy was writing a book in a week. I completed the entire draft, approximately 150 pages, over the course of three days. The chapters came back from the typist, went to the Christies for editing, from the Christies to an attorney for review, to the designer who had already put a cover together, complete with blurbs from the likes of Tyra

Banks, a close friend of Jackie's, and some of Doug's NBA friends.

Five weeks later, the Christies had their book, *No Ordinary Love*, published in hardcover, available on Amazon, and telling the true story of their relationship and the legal problems that had followed Doug from city to city … all because he wouldn't sleep with the women who were literally throwing themselves at him. As a result, the Christies transformed their image in the Seattle business community. They became respected and admired partners in the high-quality, low-income housing they wanted to provide in their neighborhoods as a way of giving back.

CHRIS MYERS

NASCAR Nation: How Racing's Values Mirror America's

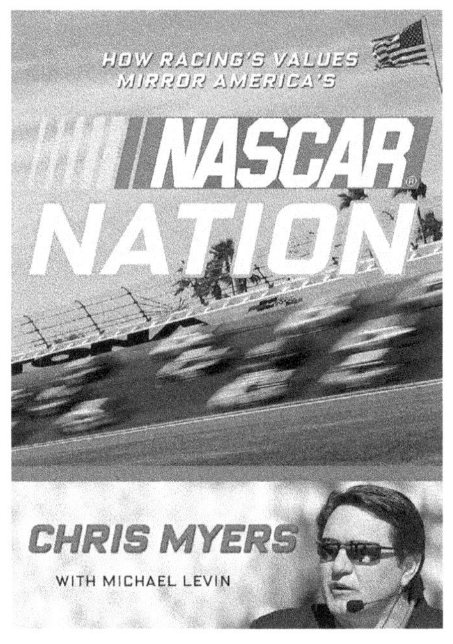

Years ago, I had an assistant who was extraordinary at cold-calling celebrities and getting them on the phone. You never knew who might want a book, and somehow, she had the incredible gift of getting past the gatekeepers, getting the private cell number, or otherwise making contact with superstars. Not all of these conversations turned into deals, of course. One time, I was getting a haircut when the receptionist at the barber shop called me to the phone.

"There is a call for you," she said, looking puzzled. "Somebody named Brian Cashman."

My assistant had somehow explained to Brian that I was getting a haircut, looked up the number for the barbershop, gave it to him, and asked him to call me there. Remarkably, he did. With half a head of hair cut and the other half uncut, I tied up the barber shop's phone line for about 20 minutes while I pitched Brian on the idea of a book. He didn't bite, but it was fun to talk with him, nevertheless.

We had more success with Chris Myers, then and now the Fox Sports broadcaster, who covers baseball, football, and auto racing. He was having so much fun doing NASCAR that the idea of a book about NASCAR appealed to him enormously. From that cold call, a book, and a friendship, grew.

You could say there are only two kinds of people in the world - people who love NASCAR and people who have never given it a second thought. I was in the second camp for most of my life, and so, quite frankly, was Chris. He was what race fans derisively called a "stick and ball guy." His expertise ran to sports that involved, well, sticks and balls, not auto racing. So when Fox Sports tapped Chris to become their lead NASCAR broadcaster, the decision caused no small amount of consternation … in NASCAR Nation.

He learned the sport quickly, and his affable, unflappable good nature went a long way toward creating trust between him and the 50 million people who love NASCAR. How much do they love NASCAR? Well, if their favorite driver switches sponsorships from Home Depot to Lowe's, they all quit shopping at Home Depot and move over to Lowe's. NASCAR fans are probably the single most tenacious, knowledgeable sports fans of any kind in the world.

You probably didn't know that, and neither did I until we wrote *NASCAR Nation*. I also didn't know much about the history of NASCAR. The races derive from moonshiners who needed fast cars to get away from the "revenuers," the legal and tax authorities who spent most of Prohibition unsuccessfully trying to shut their illegal stills down. When they weren't outgunning the cops, the rum runners would race their souped-up jalopies against each other. The races eventually were formalized, and the world of stock car racing was born.

The cars are called "stock" because, back in the day, they were manufactured from the normal stock you would find at your local Ford or Chevy dealership. Today, of course, the cars are fabricated in seemingly magic ways, much of which we detail in *NASCAR Nation*. The races were, and are, much more relatable to a wide swath of Americans compared to Formula 1 because the cars look just like the cars regular people drive, and the drivers look like regular people, too. Not your fancy European types who tend to dominate F1.

I took my kids to a NASCAR race, thanks to Chris, and they really liked the pre-race pageantry, when the cars and the pit crews would all line up for the national anthem. After that, though, the thing got really, really loud. So, we didn't stick around for the finish. Couldn't tell you who won that day, although I did get a ride a couple of days before the race in a regular car on the track at Riverside, California. The curves were so steeply banked that I felt we were driving up the side of a wall, and I really thought the car would topple over. It didn't, and NASCAR had a new reason to feel proud of itself after its world was immortalized in Chris' book.

CARSON DALY

The Links

You know Carson Daly as a television personality and *The Voice* host. The golf world knows him as a scratch player who regularly competes and wins or comes close to winning at the Pro-Am celebrity tournament at Pebble Beach.

Carson loves golf as much as or more than he loves music, which is saying something. He looks like a golfer - tall, whippet-thin, with explosive energy radiating from him. A publicist connected us because

Carson wanted to do a book about how golf had connected him with his father-in-law, a relationship that might have foundered were it not for their mutual love of golf. The book was about how golf could bring people together, hence the title, *The Links*.

I worked hard at getting a book proposal exactly right and drove to Carson's house at the northern tip of Santa Monica with a phenomenal view of the Pacific below. I will never know why, but Carson changed his mind about the project. And that is why the book *The Links* cannot be found on Amazon or at your local bookstore.

You might ask why I include a book that was never published in a book about the projects I have worked on. I guess I always wanted this one to see the light of day. Not everything works out, of course, in our professional lives or in any phase of our lives. And sometimes, it is hard to forget about the "one that got away."

That is what the Carson Daly project was, and remains, for me. I think we both felt strongly at the time that the book would capture Carson's love of golf and share it with a youthful audience that might have been inspired to pick up the game since Carson played it. And it might also have inspired others to reconnect, through golf, with family members or friends from whom they might have been estranged for whatever reason. The concept of the family feud isn't just a game show. Sometimes, family members don't speak for years, or even decades, long after they have forgotten why they originally fell out of contact. Carson's book would have been the perfect Father's Day gift, or the perfect gift at any time, to reconnect with that loved one where the relationship had, well, rolled into a bunker.

The toughest thing was that I never really got an explanation as to why the project was killed. They say that Hollywood is a place where wonderful things almost happen. Alas, that was the case with *The Links*.

PAT SUMMERALL

Giants: What I Learned About Life from Vince Lombardi and Tom Landry

Pat Summerall needs no intro-
duction. No one has broadcast
more Super Bowls, Masters
Tournaments, Wimbledon,
Fortnights, or other major
sporting events. He was the
mellifluous, understated partner
of the rambunctious, tur-
ducky-waving John Madden,
judicious with his words and
wry with his praise.

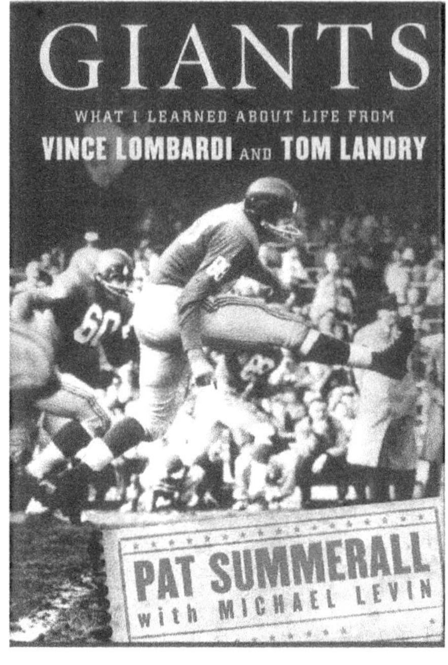

Many football fans don't know that Pat had a unique distinction
in addition to his broadcasting career - he was the only player ever
to be coached in the same season by football's two most illustrious
coaches, Vince Lombardi and Tom Landry.

Pat was a two-way player on the 1958 New York Giants, which
meant that he sat in on the defensive meetings with Tom Landry,
later lionized as the greatest head coach of his era, and the offensive
meetings with Vince Lombardi, who went on to enormous fame with
the Green Bay Packers.

I noticed that fact that Pat had been coached by both men, so
when we were introduced, I brought it up to him and suggested that
we could do a whole book about what it was like to have those two
coaches as teachers. Pat was thrilled with the idea, and we were off
and running.

Today, in the NFL, the head coach is everything. The man with
the headset and the embossed play chart, the one who gets all the
credit and takes all the blame. In 1958, Pat told me, you could walk by

the three bedrooms of the two assistant coaches and the head coach, Jim Lee Howell. All of them had rooms at the same Grand Concourse hotel where most of the players stayed, and they all kept their doors open. On an evening, you would see Lombardi and Landry hard at work on their game plans, and then you would see head coach Jim Lee Howell with his feet on the desk, reading the paper.

One of the most striking things that came out of our conversations was the manner in which Pat learned that he had been traded from the penurious Chicago Cardinals to the state-of-the-art New York Giants. He lived in his native Florida in the off-season and had gone to the post office to pick up his mail. While there, he saw a newspaper with a squib announcing that he had been traded. That is how things were, generations before ESPN and social media.

I described the Chicago Cardinals, which later became the St. Louis Cardinals, and ultimately the Arizona Cardinals as penurious, a fancy way of saying "cheap." How cheap were they? Well, Pat, his wife, and their baby lived in a single hotel room because that was all they could afford. The baby slept in an open dresser drawer. Now, *that is cheap*.

Pat also told me about the origins of the NFL Players Association, which was founded, he said, because the players were fed up with having to buy their own sneakers. That is right - the NFL Players Association, one of the most powerful unions in the world, came into existence over the lowly issue of the cost of sneakers. Pat told me that sometimes when he went into locker rooms he would see more sneakers at the locker of any one player than an entire team had back in the late 50s.

My other favorite moment from our conversations, aside from the overall thrill of talking football with the voice I knew so well from TV broadcasts and True Value Hardware ads (Just tell them Pat Summerall sent you!), was when we were talking about a preseason game played in the second week of August 1958.

I told Pat that that was the week I was born.

He chuckled, and with that languorous Florida twang, he replied, "That was a loooooooong time ago!"

TIM DONAGHY

Personal Foul: A First-Personal Account of the Scandal that Rocked the NBA

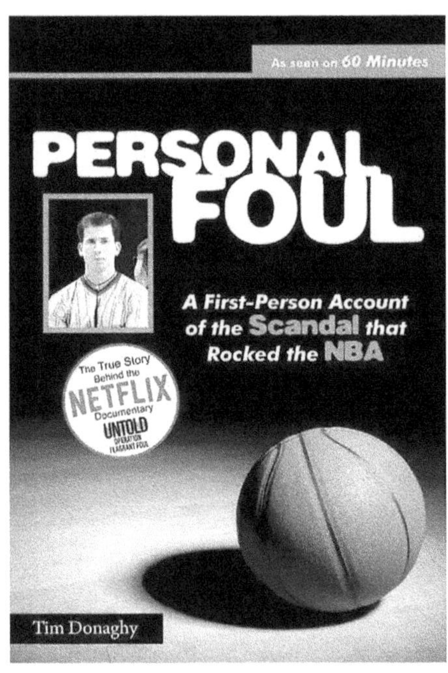

Tim Donaghy had it all -- a beautiful wife, wonderful daughters, and an enviable career as an NBA referee. Night after night, he was on the court with the greatest of them all -- Michael Jordan, Charles Barkley, Shaquille O'Neal, Kobe Bryant. He knew them, and they knew him. And the money wasn't bad, either.

And yet, for Tim, the money wasn't enough. Tim was doing a bunch of sports betting, which brought him to the attention of the Mob in Eastern Pennsylvania, where he lived. It occurred to them that Tim was useful for a lot more than a few bets on sporting events. Tim was the ultimate source of inside information for NBA games.

Everyone always sensed that the NBA wanted to see certain matchups in the playoffs, like Celtics-Lakers because that would be far more lucrative than, say, New Orleans-Utah, but no one had been able to prove exactly how the NBA got the results they wanted.

It turned out that the NBA's method of choice for ensuring those favorable outcomes was using certain members of the referee crew.

Tim started funneling information to the Mob about who he thought would win on a given night. He was the referee in some of those games, but, more significantly, he knew the League's tendencies, so he knew how to craft his own betting lines and share those with the Mob ... for a fee, of course.

Eventually, the story went public, Tim was disgraced and imprisoned for about a year, and the League, at least theoretically, cleaned up its act. Or did it?

Tim wanted to do a book that would first convey his sense of guilt and sorrow for what he had done. In addition, he wanted to force the NBA to clean up its act, and he exposed the various techniques by which the NBA got the outcomes they wanted without putting anything in writing or leaving themselves the possibility of getting caught.

They might appoint a young referee with "rabbit ears" - one who would be afraid to make a call that would rile the crowd - if the NBA wanted the home team to win.

Or the League office would send a video to the referees covering a certain game demonstrating a certain sort of foul that the League office wanted the referees to pay close attention to and call at every opportunity. It would be the kind of move that only one player on the court was known for making. This was a clear signal to the referees about which team was supposed to lose - the one with the player who made that move.

Or they would simply put a referee who was known to play ball with the League into a game, rightly convinced that the ref would make just enough subtle calls to tip the balance of the contest.

When the book came out, howls of denial issued forth from the NBA's Fifth Avenue offices. It is total fiction! How can you trust Tim Donaghy? He is a cheater!

He admitted he was a cheater, but the NBA never admitted that they were, too.

As a basketball fan, I remember sitting in my car listening to the fourth quarter of a notorious Lakers-Kings playoff game, where there were almost two dozen fouls called against the Kings in the last 15 or so minutes of play. As a result, a game that the Lakers should have lost went into their win column, and they advanced in the playoffs, much to the delight of the NBA offices.

For Tim, this game became Exhibit A in his case against the NBA.

It was riveting to listen to Tim tell the story of how he had become a referee in the first place, how Michael Jordan and Phil Jackson stormed at him on his first night after he had called a foul against Jordan - in Philadelphia, where the entire crowd was raining down boos on Tim. Why the furor from Jordan, Jackson, and the fans, Tim wondered. He later learned that the NBA didn't want Tim calling fouls on Michael Jordan. They didn't want to risk Jordan fouling out.

Welcome to the NBA, Tim. And it was even more fascinating to hear Tim explain how the NBA dictated outcomes. Referees who "played ball" would be rewarded by getting assignments, going deeper into the playoffs, making more money, or moving up faster in the ranks.

The NBA put in an entirely new system for managing the refereeing crew to ensure there would never be another Tim Donaghy. At the same time, many of the refs Tim named as the worst offenders remained in their posts and continued to deliver desirable outcomes to the League. The refs may change, but the game remains the same.

CHAD HENNINGS

Rules of Engagement: Finding Faith and Purpose in a Disconnected World

When Chad Hennings was a junior in high school in Iowa, he was competing for the state wrestling championship and lost. You might associate Iowa with baseball because of the movie *Field of Dreams*, but high school wrestling is actually the biggest sport in the state. And Chad had just gotten

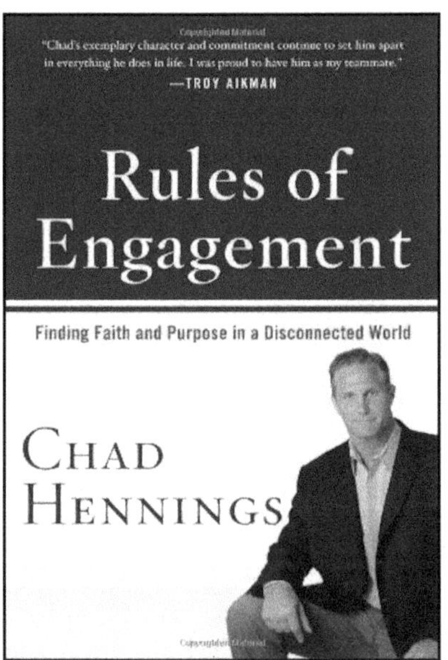

trounced even though he was bigger, taller, and stronger than the kid who had pinned him … in front of 13,000 people in the arena and millions more watching at home.

That loss triggered a gut-check moment for Chad, who worked ten times harder over the course of his senior year to get back to the finals, and this time, of course, he won. I asked him what was going through his mind as he accepted the trophy.

"So this is what it takes to succeed," he explained.

Chad took that mentality of hard work into his college football career, in which he won the Outback Award for being the premier offensive lineman in the nation. He then took that same mentality into his military career, where, during the First Gulf War, he flew dozens of humanitarian missions to the Kurds, even though at 6'4" tall, he was technically too big to fly any of the military aircraft he piloted.

And then he took that same attitude and work ethic into his first training camp with the Dallas Cowboys. Due to his military service, he was considerably older than any other rookie in camp and had to prove himself to coach Jimmy Johnson and his staff. Wasn't he too old to get started in the NFL at age 25?

The results speak for themselves. Chad won three Super Bowl rings with the Cowboys during the "triplet" days, when Troy Aikman, Michael Irvin, and Emmitt Smith deservedly received most of the glory. Chad's broad exposure to life - a celebrity in the state of Iowa thanks to his wrestling, his military career, and his NFL experience, left him with the indelible impression that in our society, men were incapable of connecting deeply or meaningfully with each other, and instead were encouraged to go it alone in whatever they did.

Chad created an organization called Wingman, one of whose weekly prayer meetings I attended while we were working on his book, *Rules of Engagement.* Chad wanted to inspire men to connect with God and one another because the most important things in life - work, family, community, spirituality - required teamwork, not a John Wayne mentality. That is why he wanted to describe his career and his religious beliefs in the book, which was published by Faith Words, one of America's leading Christian book publishers.

Chad and I remained friends, and I would come down to Dallas to go to a Cowboys game with him. One game we attended together was the celebration of the Cowboys' 50th anniversary, complete with a huge party in Jerry Jones' private suite, which is about the size of the Admirals Club at DFW. I met Roger Staubach, Bob Lilly, Hollywood Henderson, and a few dozen other legends. Staubach looked like he could still suit up and play. He looked like the cool guy at a college frat party.

Here I am with Leon Lett, Chad, and Hall of Famer Charles Haley:

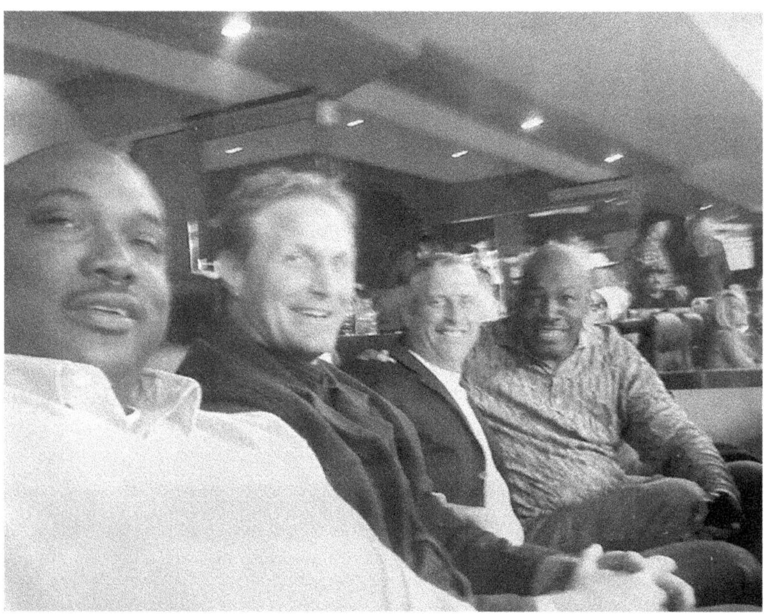

Walking around the stadium with Chad was like walking with royalty. Everybody in Dallas loves Chad Hennings, trust me. And as we encountered so many of his fans, who were so happy to see him, I got the sense that Chad loves everybody in Dallas, too.

DAVE WINFIELD

Dropping The Ball: aseball's Troubles and How We Can and Must Solve Them

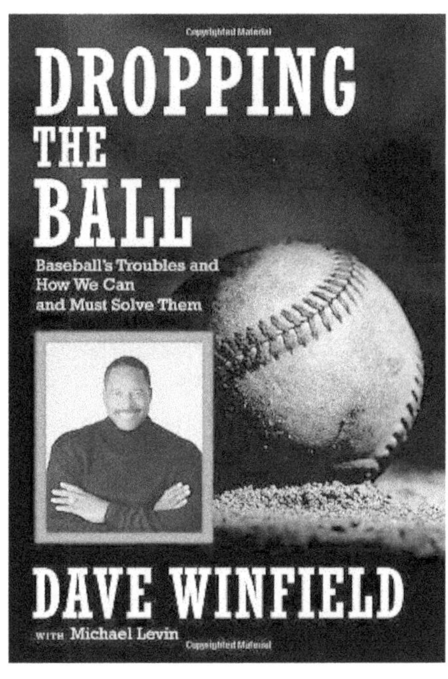

One day in 1996, a top literary agent in New York City called. He needed a ghostwriter to work with Dave Winfield, the Hall of Fame baseball star whom I had seen play for years with the Yankees and who went on to win a world series with Toronto. Would I have lunch with Dave Winfield? I'm a New York sports fan. Are you kidding me? I said of course, and he said he'd give Dave my number.

Two days later, I was leaving the office and walking to my car when my cell rang. Unknown number. It was Dave. I dropped my briefcase (I had a briefcase back then), and Dave and I spoke for 15 minutes. We made lunch plans. I couldn't believe I was going to have lunch with Baseball Hall of Famer Dave Winfield.

At lunch, we hit it off. Anybody would like Dave. He's brilliant, charming, fun, and well-aware of his role as an ambassador for the game. At that lunch, and every subsequent time we went out together in public, Dave would be accosted by fans in restaurants, on the street, in shopping malls, wherever we were. And he always gave them that easy smile and took all the time he wanted to talk about baseball. I would go to the men's room and find him holding court, surrounded by a bunch of admiring fans. I loved that about him.

I must have passed whatever the test was because, at the end of the meal, Dave reached into his attaché case and handed me a thick batch of files, hundreds of pages of notes about a book he wanted to write.

"Read this and call me and tell me what you think," he said. We shook hands and said goodbye, and I stood there watching him go, holding those hundreds of pages of material from Dave Winfield in my hands and wondering, did that just happen?

I took the pages back to my office and sat down to read. And the more I read, the more discouraged I felt. The idea of the book Dave wanted to write was simply too small. There was no way a New York publisher would take it on. So, I sketched out an idea for a book that captured Dave's core ideas while at the same time presenting them in a way that had the potential to attract a significant audience for the book.

A day later, when I had the title, subtitle, and chapter titles on paper and polished to the best of my ability, I called Dave. I explained why his idea was probably not commercial, and then I walked him through the approach I had come up with, title, subtitle, and each of the chapters.

There was a long pause. Long enough for me to contemplate the fact that I could have worked with Dave Winfield had I just done what he had proposed, and I had blown it. And then came his mellifluous baritone over the phone.

"That's good," he said. "I like it!"

And a friendship was born.

Dave made me legitimate for all the other athletes I worked with later. All athletes admired Dave, not just because he was the only athlete to be drafted by all three major professional sports: baseball, football, and basketball, but because he was a thinker. If I was good enough for Dave, I was good enough for them.

Dave was particularly interested in the question of how to increase the number of African Americans in the Major Leagues. When he played in the 1970s and 1980s, approximately 24% of the Major League baseball players were Black. By the time we wrote the book, around 2009, the number had slipped to 9%. Today, the number of African American Major League baseball players is around 6%.

Dave wanted his book to explain the reasons why fewer and fewer young Black athletes were aiming for careers in baseball. Dave, of course, is the only athlete in history ever drafted by all three professional sports—Major League Baseball, the NFL, and the NBA. When I asked him why he chose baseball over, say, being a running back, he just laughed and told me, "I didn't want to spend my life at the bottom of a pile." Why were there fewer Black Major Leaguers? Dave offered four explanations. First, baseball is an expensive sport because there is so much gear involved, and inner-city youth can't necessarily afford the bats, the gloves, the balls, the spikes, and so on.

Next, in prior decades, young people could play baseball on fields in the inner city all day long, weather permitting. Today, most of those fields have given way to mini-malls and apartment houses, so there are simply fewer places to play. On top of that, the communities are not as safe as they once were, which means that somebody's parent has to be there to watch and make sure the kids are safe. Few parents have the luxury of that kind of time since everybody has to work.

The third reason is economic. The way the baseball draft works, you can bring 10 to 15 players from the Dominican Republic to the United States to have a shot at making the team for the cost of drafting one native-born American player, Black or white. What happens to those young Dominicans who fail to make the cut is a question nobody seems to care about, Dave told me, but if you can have 15 chances on a Major Leaguer by importing prospects from the Caribbean or Latin America, that is where your scouting and development dollars go. The fourth reason Dave gave me was social. High school girls are into high school boys who play basketball and football. Baseball, these days? Not so much.

I thought about that brilliant piece of guidance I had received at the beginning of my career that no one remembers even a well-written government report. So, how could we turn Dave's concern for the future of Blacks in Major League Baseball, and the reasons we discussed, into a way that would be memorable and a conversation topic for when Dave promoted the book?

The answer I came up with was the concept of "The Last Black Major Leaguer." He said that based on the trends, social and economic, it was entirely possible that somewhere in the United States, some six-year-old boy with a love of baseball would be the "Last Black Major Leaguer," end of story. We created a profile of this youngster. We suggested he lived in Florida, Arizona, or Southern California, where baseball was prevalent and could be played most of the year. We talked about his socioeconomic background and all the other factors we could think of. Our composite portrait of the "Last Black Major Leaguer" became a chapter in the book and, indeed, became one topic the media found fascinating.

The book was called *Dropping the Ball: Baseball's Troubles and How We Can and Must Solve Them*. It was a national bestseller, and I'm especially proud of the fact that the legendary Hank Aaron blurbed the book. Dave wrote some nice things about me in the acknowledgments section and concluded by saying, "I guess my draft choice for a co-writer paid off."

SECTION 6

MORE BOOKS I LOVE

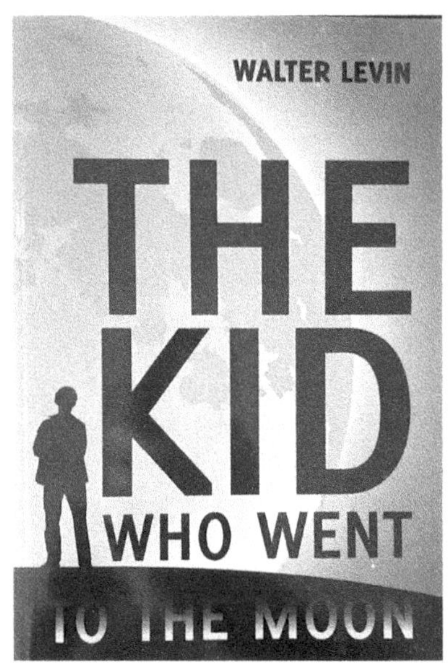

WALTER LEVIN

The Kid Who Went to the Moon

When my son Walter was 12, we were on a cross-country flight, and he told me that he was going to start writing a novel, so he needed to borrow my laptop. He pounded away and then, after the trip, continued occasionally to return to his manuscript. A couple of months later, he told me that the book was done, and he wanted me to read it.

I felt a sense of misgiving. How do you tell your 12-year-old son that his novel is just okay? To my surprise and delight, *The Kid Who Went to the Moon* had energy, humor, bounce, and a professionalism way beyond his years. I didn't teach him anything. He just figured everything out for himself.

The short novel tells the story of, well, a kid who goes to the moon. He fundraises, he tinkers, he bangs, and he creates a spaceship. On the moon, he encounters strange creatures and comes home safely. My company published the book, and Walter even had a book signing at a privately owned bookstore in West Los Angeles. Today, he's 21, and he continues to write books. But it all started with *The Kid Who Went to the Moon.*

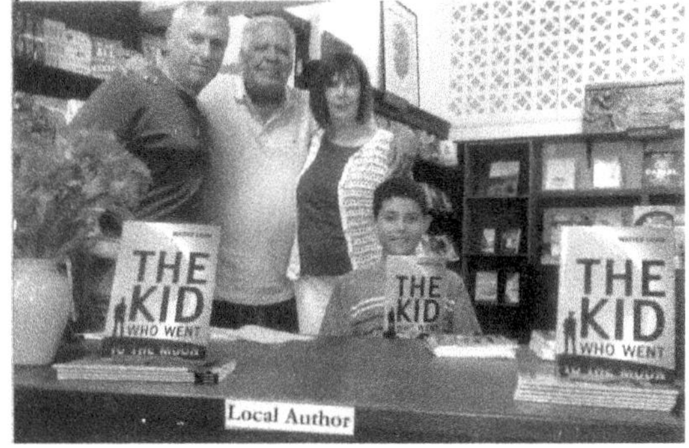

Walter Levin, age 11, at his first book signing, Los Angeles, California, 2014

SHENESKA JACKSON

Caught Up in the Rapture

In 1988, a very dear friend, the late Debbie Berger, invited three of her writer friends to dinner. One was an Emmy-winning screenwriter with whom I am still close to this day. Another taught in the UCLA writer's program, then and now the gold standard for teaching writing, whether we are talking about movies, TV, or books. And the third was this kid named Michael Levin, who had sold a few novels to Simon & Schuster. I had just come out to Los Angeles that summer to take a screenwriting course at the UCLA writer's program with the legendary Lew Hunter, widely recognized as one of the top screenwriting profs on the planet.

So, imagine my considerable surprise when, a few weeks later, I received a call from the head of the UCLA writer's program asking me if I would like to come teach there. That was one of those "nearly fell off my chair" moments. Of course, the answer was yes, and I ended up teaching at UCLA for more than 17 years.

When I taught my writing classes at UCLA, New York University, around the country, and eventually around the world, I always made my students the same offer. When you complete a manuscript, send me the first 50 double-spaced pages. If I fall in love with it, I will move heaven and earth to get you a literary agent and a publisher.

The publishing world was different back then. The major houses bought, say, a dozen first novels a year, including Simon & Schuster's purchase of my first novel back in 1986. Today, you have to sell thousands of copies of multiple novels independently before New York will even give you a sniff; however, back then, the publishing houses were looking for promising young writers. I was connected to the New York publishing world pretty tightly back then, and I had connections, so the offer I made to my students was no joke.

I'm happy to report that more than half a dozen of my students went on to have careers as bestselling authors. The one I want to tell you about is Sheneska Jackson. Sheneska was a student of mine at UCLA. She worked in the Health Department of the City of Los Angeles. She would come home at night, play a couple of hours of Tetris, and then get to work on her novel, *Caught Up in the Rapture*, set in South Los Angeles, where she had grown up.

Sheneska took me up on my offer, and I thought those first 50 pages were solid gold. I called her and asked if she could make a couple of changes to one of the subplots. Two days later, a package arrived at my door with the changes made. There was nothing else to say. I turned the manuscript over to a literary agent I knew, who fell in love with it. She sent it to an editor at Simon & Schuster, who read the manuscript while she was on jury duty. And from a flip phone in the jurors' holding area, that editor, Mary Ann Naples, called Sheneska - this was way before cell phones were a "thing" - and offered her $200,000 for a two-book deal.

Suddenly, Sheneska went from being a clerk in the City of LA's health system to becoming one of the highest-paid Black women fiction writers in America.

My reward came nine months later when the book came out, and Sheneska received a two-page color spread in People magazine.

Sheneska didn't need my class. She was already everything a great writer needed to be. When I asked her why she took the class, she said that she thought the novel was good, but she just wanted to make sure she wasn't missing anything.

Trust me, she wasn't missing anything at all.

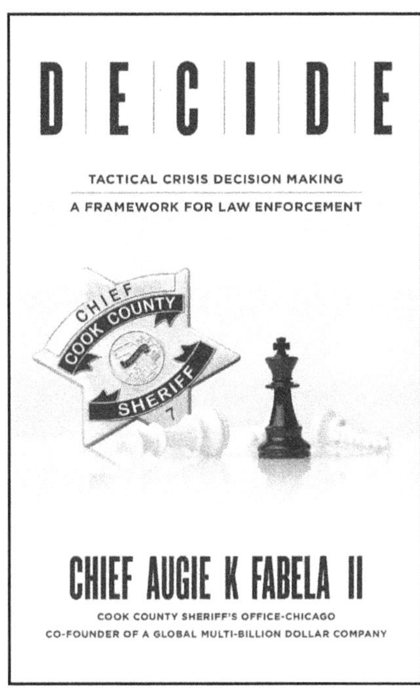

AUGIE FABELA II

D.E.C.I.D.E.—Tactical Crisis Decision Making: A Framework For Law Enforcement

When Augie Fabela II went to Moscow in 1992 to found a telecom firm, Boris Yeltsin had just taken over, Russia was reeling from the collapse of communism, the mafia ruled the streets, and businessmen were literally getting shot left and right. Into this maelstrom sailed Augie, whose company began offering early cell phones - the size and shape of large bricks - for $5,000 a unit, cash on the barrelhead. The company quickly took off, and Augie noticed that certain working women in certain entertainment neighborhoods were among his best customers. He knew this because prostitutes did most of their work in Moscow on Friday and Saturday nights, and that is where their calls were coming in.

At one point, members of the Russian mafia demanded a cut of the action in a midnight meeting held in a cemetery. Somehow, Augie and his team said no (and survived). He then expanded his company into other places where most businesspeople would fear to tread. Kyrgyzstan. Pakistan. African nations unserved by the bigger firms. Eventually, Augie's company became the seventh-largest telecom in the world and the first Russian-based company to be listed on the New York Stock Exchange since before the 1917 Soviet Revolution. Augie himself became the youngest CEO in the history of the New York Stock Exchange to ring the bell when he took his company public.

Augie realized that there's a huge overlap between the skills that make businesspeople successful and the skills that make law enforcement effective. In addition to the businesses he runs, Augie serves as one of the leaders of the Cook County Sheriff's Department, one of the entities responsible for policing the city of Chicago. I edited a book Augie wrote called *D.E.C.I.D.E.*, which offers a business-based framework for law enforcement agencies to deploy their resources and get the best result. The focus is on how you make high-stakes decisions under pressure. In the business world, the results affect the bottom line; in policing, high-stakes decisions are matters of life and death.

His book lays out a business-inspired approach to community policing that has brought down the number of shooting deaths in the South Side of Chicago and has been documented to have worked everywhere else where it has been implemented. What qualifies Augie to serve as Cook County Sheriff and guide other law enforcement departments? I suppose that if you can survive Yeltsin's Moscow, you can handle just about anything.

SUZY MILLER

Awesomism!: A New Way to Understand the Diagnosis of Autism

Three words parents fear when they speak to their pediatrician about a child whose behavior is hard to understand or manage are 'on the spectrum.' The phrase brings fear into the hearts of parents because of the

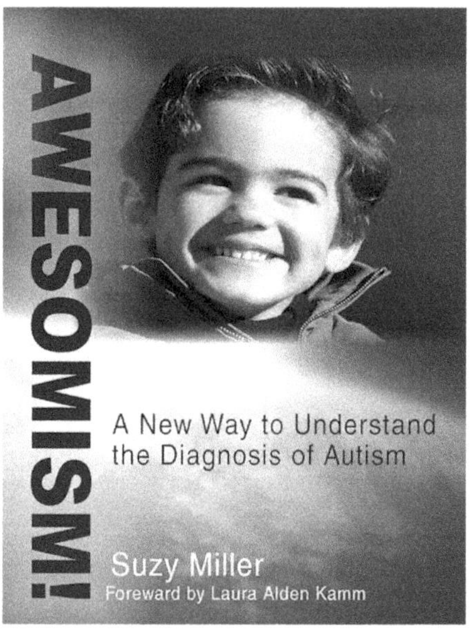

confusion, upset, and, frankly, terror that the diagnosis of autism so often provokes. As with many other diagnoses in a society practically controlled by Big Pharma, the most common way to treat autism is with drugs.

But what if you don't want to drug your child up? What if you want to see a child with autism as unique and precious, not broken? And what if you would like to find a way to move your child off the autism spectrum permanently, without pharmaceuticals?

Suzy Miller is a practitioner who treats children with autism but sees them in a very different light from most medical doctors. She doesn't even like the term autism, preferring "Awesome!" instead because, in her experience, these kids are just so awesome. Suzy found explanations for their unusual clusters of behavior and ways to understand in spiritual terms where these kids were coming from. As a result, Suzy has been able to help parents of children with autism find alternative treatments that don't require drugs.

Now, pharmaceuticals have their place. There are times when drugs are absolutely the right course, but something is amiss when pharmaceutical companies have such massive marketing and advertising budgets and when doctors have little time to "get under the hood" with patients and instead reach instinctively for their prescription pads. It was my privilege to work with Suzy to help bring alternative approaches to the fore.

ROBERT H. BLUMENFIELD

Blanc de Chine: The Great Porcelain of Dehua and A Collector's Odyssey

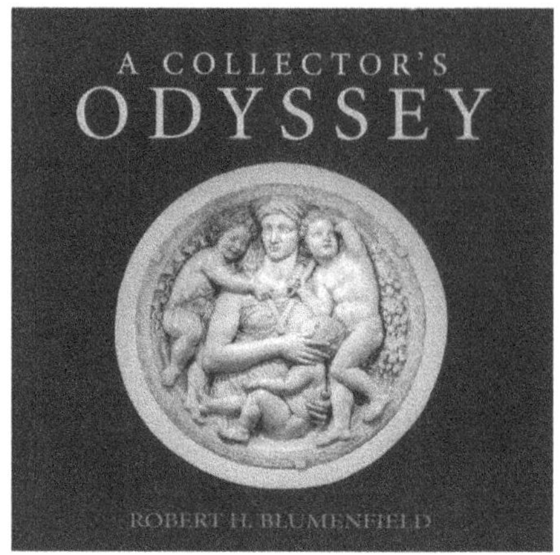

When Robert Blumenfield was 10, his mother took him to the Brooklyn Museum. Dazzled by the masterpieces that surrounded him, young Robert decided that one day, he would live in a museum, one of his own making. And that is exactly what happened. Robert went on to become one of the most successful real estate owners in Southern California, and along the way, he became an expert in art. He fell in love with a particular form of Chinese porcelain called Blanc de Chine and developed one of the world's leading collections of those dazzling porcelain figures. His interest in art far exceeded Chinese porcelain, however. He also became an authority and collector in the worlds of European art and furniture.

Almost 20 years ago, Robert became dissatisfied with the dating process for Blanc de Chine. Instead, he cultivated his own approach and brought me in to do the first of two books on art. It took us more than a year to write what has since become the definitive book on Blanc de Chine. By the end of the process, I probably knew as much about the sculptures, manufactured in the Ming and Qing dynasties, roughly from 1400 to 1750, as many experts! The book laid out Robert's unique approach to dating Blanc de Chine pieces. On a February afternoon, I visited Robert at his home, and together, we went through approximately one hundred pieces of centuries-old Chinese porcelain, passing the pieces back and forth and arguing between the two of us as to which quarter of which century each piece belonged. An experience I will never forget.

The second book we did detailed not just 50 of his favorite works of art from his collection but also his unique approach to buying art. Robert had created a broad range of dealers, auction houses, experts, and collectors who would call him out of the blue and offer him a piece. Robert would take all the information he had been given and cogitate deeply on the piece, trying to determine its uniqueness, its value, and most importantly, its greatness. Robert only wanted the greatest pieces in whatever field he was collecting. It could be agonizing for him to crunch the data that he had been given about a particular piece and then come up with an appropriate offer. On one occasion, he was taking part by phone in an art auction while sitting on a plane that was about to take off. The bidding had not concluded when the flight attendant announced that the door had been closed and it was time to terminate all conversations. Robert, panicked, told the auction house that he was to have the piece no matter what. He then spent the entire flight, in pre-Wi-Fi days, agonizing, waiting for news of whether he had won or not.

He had. And yes, his house did look like a museum!

DANIEL S. MISHKIN

The Other Side of the Bed: What Patients Go Through and What Doctors Can Learn

Daniel and Barry Mishkin had it all figured out. The brothers, separated by only a few years of age, would both complete medical school and go into practice together. Nothing would interfere with that plan, or so they thought. Barry was a beloved chief resident

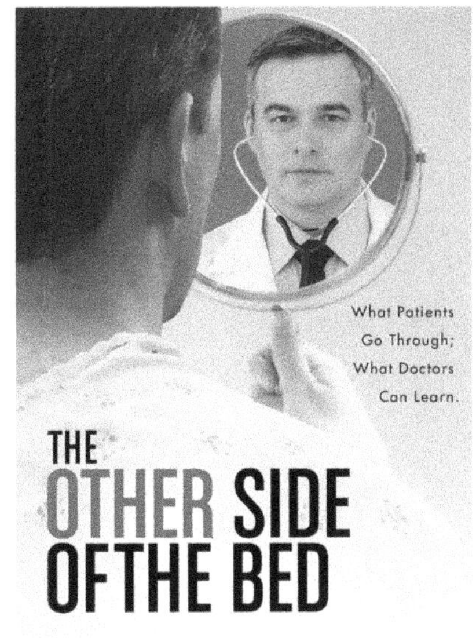

with Daniel a few years behind him in med school when Barry came down with a rare and very difficult-to-treat form of leukemia. For the next three years, Daniel became Barry's chief caregiver. As a result, he received the kind of medical education that few doctors ever experience - he learned what patient care is like from "the other side of the bed."

Getting Barry cared for, even in hospitals where Daniel had privileges due to his status as a doctor, proved incredibly difficult. Most doctors, Daniel writes, have absolutely no idea of what a maze the world of medical care is for patients and caregivers. Barry sadly passed away from leukemia after three years. Daniel, seeking to find meaning in his brother's loss, wrote the book, which I had the privilege of editing so he could lecture in medical schools on the topic of the patient experience of healthcare. Daniel has now taught multiple generations of medical school students how to have a greater level of compassion and understanding for patients and their families. These folks aren't just diagnoses or insurance codes. They are living, breathing, often suffering individuals who need compassion and empathy as much as they need the next procedure or pill.

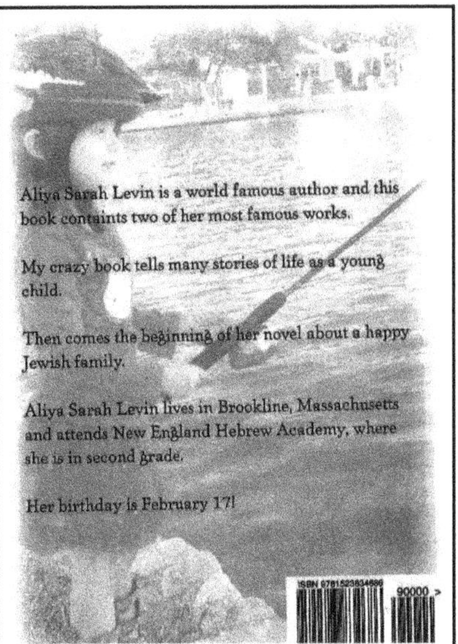

MY CRAZY BOOK

Aliya Sarah Levin

When you're a dad, and you run a company involved with books, it's fun when your kids get interested in writing. When my youngest daughter Aliya was eight years old, instead of reading before bedtime, I would be on my laptop, and she would dictate the next page or two of a book she was writing. My company ended up publishing it under the title of *My Crazy Book*. She was, and I hope, very proud of the accomplishment.

She takes particular delight in the fact that she donated the book to the Brookline Public Library, since we were living in Brookline, Massachusetts at the time, and they put it in their Local Author's Collection. So, if you happen to visit the Brookline Public Library during library hours, you can go see Aliya's book. It's under glass, along with all the other books by Brookline authors.

FINAL THOUGHTS – AND NOW IT'S YOUR TURN

I hope that the stories you have encountered in this book have inspired you to think about your life story and the meaning it conveys. As I said at the outset, my goal has not been to make anyone jealous because of the outsized success of some of the people I've written about, but instead, to make you ponder your life's meaning and decide which of the six categories of human needs best encompasses your life experience. I want to tell you two more stories before we go.

The first is of a highly successful business executive in his late 40s who had it all—a wonderful marriage, great kids, and a successful business. By now, you have seen enough Lifetime movies to suspect that this story doesn't end well, and unfortunately, it does not. He was diagnosed with a brain tumor and was given a life expectancy of under 12 months. He came to me because he wanted to capture his life lessons, not just for his children but also for his business associates and for anyone else who would care to read them. He wouldn't pull the trigger on the agreement, and I asked him why.

"If something happens to me," he said, "And the book isn't finished, I will be saddling them with another expenditure that they will have to pay off. No offense."

"No offense taken," I replied. I proposed that we make the deal on the condition that, should he pass at any time during the writing of the book, I would complete it with his family members at no additional charge. Whatever he had paid already would be considered the complete fee. His family would have no further financial obligation to me, but I would remain obligated to them to complete the project.

This was the only way I could think of to solve a problem. Unfortunately, he didn't want to take advantage of the offer, and the book was never written. We have stayed in touch, and as I write these pages, I have reached out to him, but I haven't heard back.

And now, the last story.

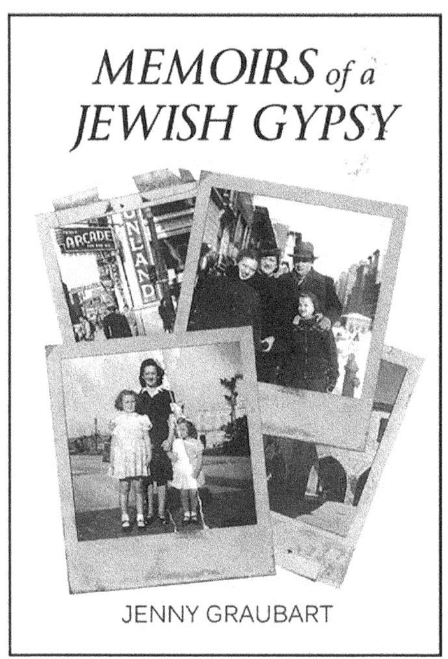

My mother, Jenny Graubart, was diagnosed with early-onset Alzheimer's when she was in her early 70s. Her family had an amazing story. She was born in Belgium in 1936, three years before the beginning of World War II. My grandfather, a Polish Jew, who had somehow fled from Poland to Czechoslovakia to Belgium when he was just 12, decided that the rising Nazi storm would be anything unlike the Jews of Europe had ever seen. So he started running from Belgium to France, the family smuggled into Spain in a hay wagon, and then via ship from Barcelona to Havana, where they spent the next six years. Finally, in 1946, the family was admitted as legal citizens into the United States.

I did not want to lose those memories to Alzheimer's.

I sensed that someone else might get more details out of my mother than I might, so I had one of the writers on my team interview my mother at length. A lot of things happened later on that she would not have wanted in the book—the murder of her father, another long story, the death of her mother from breast cancer, but really a broken heart when she lost her husband, and then my parents' divorce. It was obvious that none of those things wanted to make their way into print.

So we did a memoir of her life focusing just on the years from 1936, when she was born in Belgium, until 1946, when the family first arrived in the United States. She called herself "Jenny the Jewish Gypsy" because she had moved so many times, living in five countries before her fifth birthday, for example, and that is what we called the book.

We published the book when my kids were really too young to know her. In 2018, after having a stroke, my mother was nearing the end. Two weeks before she passed, my twin sons, then 17 years old, and I went to her apartment, which was right around the corner from our home, to visit. She slept for the entire time that we were in the house, but I will never forget—or at least I hope I never forget—the memory of seeing my sons sitting quietly in the living room, each engrossed in a copy of their grandmother's memoirs.

They will always have her story because we captured it in a book, and they will always know the courage that her family displayed in all their years on the run.

So now the question becomes, what about you? What is your life? What matters most to you? What needs to be preserved as part of your legacy for your family, friends, colleagues, team members, and future generations? There is no law that says you have to do a book, but there is no better way to capture those memories, those stories, now and forever.

Books are never a priority. So often, they fall victim to the tyranny of the urgent—the deal that needs to close, the trip that must be taken, the purchase that cannot wait. All I can do is hope this book has spurred you to recognize the value in your story so that you will consider sharing it, if not with the whole world, then with your world.

I hope you found these stories meaningful and inspiring. I specifically hope that they inspire you to ask, "What is meaningful to me?" And I hope that once you've identified the area that means the most to you – whether it's one of the ten domains I suggested or something else entirely – you want to write a book about it.

We all know the cliches – no one ever saw a hearse towing a U-Haul. Or the old line, "How much money did so-and-so leave? All of it." Our legacies must be more than financial. Buddhism teaches that when we reach a certain age and level of success, we have a responsibility to the generations that follow to share with them what we've learned and what matters most to us.

If the idea of capturing the ideas, experiences, creations, and gifts in book form appeals to you, I hope you'll reach out. You don't have to have specific ideas about the structure of the book, what's included, or what's left out. We'll work out those things together! The main thing is that you desire to share with your loved ones, friends, and colleagues … or perhaps a much bigger audience … what creates meaning in your life. If I can be useful, it will be a privilege for my team and me to serve you.

BONUS SECTION – FICTION WRITING: THE SHORT COURSE

In 1992, Kathi Goldmark was a San Francisco book publicist who had the happy coincidence of working with both Stephen King and Dave Barry in the same month. Curiously, they both confessed the same fantasy. Yes, they were thrilled that they were rock-star best-selling authors, but what they really dreamt of … was being real live rock stars.

Kathi had an idea. She reached out to a few other authors, including Amy Tan, who wrote *The Joy Luck Club,* and Barbara Kingsolver, author of *The Bean Trees* and many other great novels, and invited them to join her in a new venture. It would be a rock and roll band called the Rock Bottom Remainders. Remainders are books that nobody buys and that end up being sold for pennies on the dollar at bookstores.

All the authors loved the idea, and the band, aided by "real" musicians like Al Kooper, had its first performance at a book industry conference that year. The experience was so enjoyable for all concerned that the group decided to tour. At each stop along the way, they would invite local authors to join in as the chorus. And guess who got to do exactly that when the group came to Cambridge, Massachusetts later that year?

I knew Kathi because of my books, and she invited me to be one of the local authors for two performances at a club called Sound Stage not from the Harvard campus. The night before, she had me drive out to North Hampton, Massachusetts, to see the band for myself and to start learning the songs. After the show, I got to hang out with the authors, shoot pool with Amy Tan, and otherwise do things that were far above my station, given my lack of fame. On the drive back to Boston, I kept pulling over so I could see the notes I had made on lyrics for songs like Wooly Bully and other rock classics. Roy Blunt, Jr., the humorist, had given me the short course in the lyrics. This was decades before YouTube, of course, so I had to learn those songs on the fly. Or, more accurately, while driving. Probably not the safest thing, but I was so excited that I could have flown home. I didn't even need the car.

I survived the drive, learned the lyrics, and made two blissful appearances with the band (that's me on the far right, in the white suit).

From left – Kathi Kamen Goldmark, Al Kooper on keyboard, Amy Tan, Dave Barry, Stephen King, two more writers, Ridley Pearson (with his back to the audience). Roy Blount, Jr., Michael Levin, and behind Michael, Barbara Kingsolver

Between shows, I had one of the greatest experiences any writer could dream of: I got some alone time with Stephen King on the group's tour bus. By then, I was teaching writing three times a year at UCLA and several times a week in my own private classes. So, on behalf of my students, I asked Stephen (if I may call him by his first name in this recounting) about his method for organizing his novels.

He shook his head.

"I don't do any real organizing," he said. "I don't do an outline. I will just write two drafts and a polish, and along the way, I'll write myself notes like, 'remember to explain how Billy got the money for the airplane.'"

Rockin' out on Wooly Bully with humorist and fellow backup singer Roy Blount, Jr.

I was over the moon. What he said sounded so … Stephen King! How did Billy get the money for the airplane? Billy is a boy's name. What is a boy doing with an airplane? Well, you would have to read whatever novel King was referencing to find out.

He also said something that was probably one of his go-to jokes whenever he talked to people about writing:

"My secret of my writing is that I have the heart of an eight-year-old. I keep it in a jar on my desk."

Rim shot.

I have told that story countless times in fiction classes I have taught, at UCLA, at New York University, at conferences for attorneys who wanted to write fiction (there is a stretch!), and at writers' groups around the world.

The author with Stephen King, 1992

What I tell them is this: "If you can write a 1,000-page manuscript without an outline and then do a second draft and a polish, you certainly don't need my writing class! But if you are mortal and a regular human being, then what we talk about might be useful." And then I would explain the perennial debate about writing classes, namely, can fiction writing be taught? I will share with you now what I told my students and what I believe to this day. You cannot teach people to be talented, but you can teach talented people aspects of structure, which will allow their creativity to flow freely. The great writers, like the ones in the Rock Bottom Remainders, including Stephen King, Amy Tan, Dave Barry, Barbara Kingsolver, Ridley Pearson, and so on, all basically intuited somewhere along the way how to structure stories, acts, and scenes.

The rest of us need to be shown an approach to story structure that will actually make sense and allow us to write happily and fluidly. Then, I would take them through three types of structure—story structure, three act structure, and scene structure—over the course of a full day. This is the approach I use when I am constructing a novel or fable for my clients (or for myself). We would do the process as a group exercise. Amazingly, the approach never failed to yield a really fun and compelling story. This was true whether I was talking to adults in a UCLA Writing Program classroom, at NYU, or in a ballroom full of attorneys who wanted to be the next John Grisham. I will share the short course in these three types of structure so you can maximize your creative gifts and have a lot more fun writing.

The starting point is that organizing and writing are two completely different skills. Organizing is essentially a left-brain task, while writing is a creative, right-brain task. Your brain does not like to be asked to shunt back and forth from one hemisphere to the other. In fact, the more you do so, the more likely you are to experience pain, which is the body's way of telling you to stop doing whatever you are doing. Most people incorrectly interpret such a headache as writer's block. It is not writer's block; it is simply your brain telling you to stop pinballing back and forth between organizing and writing, between left brain and right brain, and instead, do one and then the other.

Of course, writer's block has its benefits. You can go to any bar, sit there long enough nursing a drink, and then explain to some toothsome stranger that you are a writer but you have writer's block. The sympathy you gain can usually be translated into a night of romance.

You're welcome.

Along these lines, sometimes people ask me if I ever get writer's block. "Of course not!" I exclaim with mock indignity. "I have writer's mortgage!"

But back to our topic. The takeaway is to organize first, and then write. Your brain will be happier, and you will be much more productive. I actually learned this lesson in my first-year course on legal writing from the legal writing textbook by Moynihan. So, Mr. Moynihan, if you are still out there, I thank you.

The first aspect of structure we will consider is story structure. In other words, how do you come up with a character and a plot that will be interesting enough to you so that you will carry through all the way to the end of the draft instead of developing what I call "half-finished novel in a drawer syndrome"—a non-fatal, but nevertheless miserable condition that afflicts writers who organize and write at the same time (not you, or not you any longer). I offer my students a five-step process as follows:

1. *Premise.* Novels and fables are means by which we seek to convince readers of a perspective on something. As Erica Jong once said at an Author's Guild Conference I organized in Los Angeles, "Our job as writers is to rearrange the molecules in the reader's brain." In other words, the reader might not have ever thought about a topic or might think about it in a way contrary to what we believe. Our job is to convince them to think about the topic just as we see it. So we are not writing about themes. We are not writing novels about love, war, or

topics. Instead, we are making points: love is the most import-ant thing in the world. Love is a lie. War is always terrible. War is sometimes necessary. What is your point of view? What is your argument? What do you want people to come away with after they have read the story? That is the first thing you want to think about, and everything else follows. Is this the only way to organize a story? No, but it works. It works really well. So let's keep going.

2. *Character.* What character would you like to choose to illus-trate the premise you chose in step one? The good news, I tell my students, is that virtually any character can illustrate vir-tually any premise. Let's stick with "love is the most beautiful thing in the world" because it is so positive and fun. To illus-trate this premise, we could choose a man, a woman, an older person, a younger person, what have you as a main character. I always like "odometer birthdays," any birthday that has a nine in it, because people tend to get more thoughtful about their lives when the odometer is about to turn over and they are hitting 20, 30, 40, and so on. So, let's make our main char-acter a 29-year-old woman named Jennie. Why Jennie? Why not? Your job as a writer is to keep making decisions. The only wrong decision you can make is the decision not to make the next decision. You can always unmake decisions later. Most writers freeze at the idea of making a decision. This translates into writer's block. Just keep making the next decision. That is the ticket to success.

Sometimes I will ask my students, "Who here has read a bad book?" Laughter followed by hands going up. "Who has ever seen a bad TV show or a bad movie?" More laughter. More hands go up.

"What do all these bad books, TV shows, and movies have in common?" I ask.

People look confused. They don't know.

"They all got finished," I said. "The people who wrote them may not have been great writers, but they finished what they started. As a result, they had something to show and something to sell. It doesn't matter how good you are if you don't finish. And the only way you can finish is by making the next decision in front of you."

So, we are going to make some decisions about Jennie. We said she is 29. She comes from a farm in Iowa. She had a lonely childhood. Her parents are divorced. And so on. You fill in the rest of the blanks. Ideally, you want to write at least a paragraph and maybe a full double-spaced page about her, so you can see her in your mind's eye. This leads to our next step, because if you only have a character description, you don't have a story.

3. *Desire.* People have to want things for a story to be successful and for a character to be compelling. So, you must ask, "What does my character want?" At this point, I have explained to the students that there are three basic "food groups" of human desire: love, security, and society. By love, I mean the love of an individual, spouse, partner, child, parent, pet, rose garden … what have you. So, you have to ask, what desire does my character have in terms of love?

Next, security. People want to feel secure. There are all kinds of security; financial, emotional, job, spiritual, and so on. What kind of security does your character lack, and what would she like to achieve?

A third "food group" of human desire is society. People want to belong. This is especially true when we are so isolated by technology and social media. Some people don't just want to belong to society; they also want to lead it or dominate it. So now, you have the three food groups. My suggestion is that you endow your main character with a desire from each of these three groups: love, security, and society. If you only pick one, the story will be "linear," which is a kiss of death word in the publishing industry. Instead, you want somebody to tap your manuscript thoughtfully and say the magic word, "complexity." A story doesn't have to be overly complex, but if you are giving your character three different desires instead of one, you will have a complex enough story.

Jennie is 29 and wants to get married, but she is very shy. That is a challenge for her. In terms of security, she came from a very religious background, but she has trouble believing in God. So, she would like to establish some sort of spiritual security. This will tie into her relationship with her father, which will tie into her challenges in finding a successful relationship. And then, in terms of society, we mentioned a moment ago that she is shy. She moves to Des Moines, which is a relatively big city for someone coming from a farm town. She feels isolated. She wants to belong.

Where did I get all this stuff from? I just made it up, but suddenly, we have a much more robust view of Jennie because we understand what she wants, and we have given her three different desires that will intertwine over the course of the story. This leads to our next step, because if a character could simply achieve everything they want with a snap of the fingers, we don't have much of a story, do we?

4. *Conflict.* For each desire, there must be an equal and opposite conflict standing in the way. Why are you going opposite? A football fan might like the Dallas Cowboys and his hometown football team, but he doesn't want to see them play each other (or maybe he is weird and he does!). We want to see the conflicting elements *in rough balance.* This means the Dallas Cowboys are playing, say, the San Francisco 49ers, and your high school football team is playing the next town's high school football team. That is a fair fight. In our case, let's give Jennie a conflict that matches her desires. She wants to be married, but she is so shy that she finds it very hard to connect enough with another person to forge a meaningful bond. She wants to have a spiritual life, but she struggles with the religious upbringing her parents gave her (inflicted on her?). She wants to be a part of things in Des Moines, but like many of us today, she has no idea how to make any kind of meaningful connection with

other people. She does not know how to escape her isolation. The story is getting more complicated, wouldn't you agree?

5. *Risk.* The final element of our story creation template is risk, and I tell my students there are really only two kinds of risk in the world. There is "going for it" risk and there is "not going for it" risk. The not going for it risk is always the same thing—you feel lonely, miserable, and unfulfilled. Sort of like a writer who doesn't follow their destiny and start writing! By contrast, the going for it risk will vary, but it must be huge. For Jennie to overcome her shyness, spiritual challenges, and inability to connect and form community, well, that is going to be a very big lift. She knows she is going to risk rejection and a sense of failure if she "goes for it." But she must. Your character always goes for it. Otherwise, what was the point of even doing this much work? We create stories by thinking through, in order, premise, character, desire, conflict, and risk. And then we see what the story is by looking at it this way: character, desire, conflict, risk, premise. Which leaves us with this: Jennie, 29, has left her hometown, a farming community in Iowa, and moved to Des Moines. She wants to get married, she wants to have a healthy relationship with God or a higher power, and she desperately wants to be part of a community. She feels so lonely. She finds opportunities to move forward in all these areas … she finds the courage and goes for it. Thus, she illustrates the premise that "love is the most beautiful thing in the world."

Now, this may sound like a Lifetime movie to you, but those Lifetime movies make a lot of money! You should be so lucky, as they say. Obviously, this is a somewhat corny example, but if you work through these five steps, you might just come up with something you find really thrilling and authentic. So, I will leave you to do just that.

Now, let's talk about the second phase of structure, three act structure. I'm borrowing this from Syd Field's book, *Screenplay*, as well as the brilliance of my own writing teacher, Lew Hunter, whom

I first met in 1988 when I drove across country to take his screenwriting class. I will preface this section by saying that I am only talking about American storytelling. Other places in the world have different approaches, but this is what we are used to here in America.

I will keep it simple and brief. Stories break down into three acts: a beginning, a middle, and an ending. The beginning and the ending are typically each 25% of the story, and the middle section is roughly 50%. Between acts one and two, and then between acts two and three are what Syd Field calls plot points, moments so huge that no scene that precedes the plot point could move into the following act, or vice versa. Also, act one is what I call "meet the people." We find out who is in the story and what kind of story it will be. Act two is the complications that flow from the first plot point or turning point in the story. Act three is the conclusion, and it flows from the plot point of the conclusion of act two.

I know I threw a lot of theory at you, so let's put it in practical terms with the movie I always use at this point in my class—*The Wizard of Oz.*

Act one—meet the people. Dorothy. Toto. The Professor. A storm is brewing in Kansas.

Plot point one—the tornado blows the house to Oz.

Act two (helpfully in color) so that writing students forever more will understand that this is act two—Oz. Dorothy's quest—to get back home. The complications that ensue from plot point one— she killed one Wicked Witch, so she has enemies. She has to get the broomstick. She meets the Cowardly Lion, the Tin Man, and the Scarecrow. And off they go to get to the Wizard, so she can get home.

Plot point two, dividing act two from act three—some may differ, but I say it is the moment when they enter the lair of the Wizard. And this takes us to the conclusion, when (spoiler alert) we find out it was all a dream.

To go slightly more deeply, in act three, there are actually three scenes (I will define what a scene is in a moment) that are practically obligatory in American storytelling. If you leave them out, your readers (or moviegoers) will say, "The story was great, but the ending was flat." It is simply because you didn't provide them with the three scenes that they expect in every act three. They are as follows, and always in this order:

1. The Big Gloom. Sometimes my students mishear me and think that I said the Big Goon or Big Groom. No, it is the Big Gloom. This is the moment when all appears lost. For Dorothy, it is the moment she realizes that the man behind the curtain is not really a Wizard. Now, she will never get home.

2. Mano a Mano—this is the dramatic scene between the two main characters, a moment of conflict that could never have occurred if we hadn't had everything in the story prior to this moment. Everything leads us to this conflict. In the Mano a Mano in the Wizard of Oz, Dorothy is having it out with the Wizard, who convinces her that she already has everything she needs inside of her. Coincidentally, that is the premise of the entire movie—you already have what you need (think about it).

And this leads to the third element of a successful act three: the amazing ending. An amazing ending is one where the audience simply says, "Oh, wow! That was amazing!" She clicks her heels … ruby slippers … it is all a dream … and you were in it … the end. And that is three act structure.

Because I'm teaching fiction writing and not screenwriting, I follow up by illustrating John Updike's magnificent novel, *Rabbit, Run*. Updike was in his early 20s when he wrote *Rabbit, Run*, which, for my money, is one of the best pieces of fiction ever written in English. By the way, *Rabbit, Run* has 10 scenes in the first act, 20 in the second act, and 10 in the third act. John Grisham novels have 20 in the first act, 40 in the second act, and 20 in the third act. Robert Ludlum novels have 40, 80, and 40.

How do I know? Because I counted the scenes in each of those books. (And in many, many more, when I was teaching myself to write novels.) Those numbers illustrate the fact that typically acts one and three are short and act two is long.

Back to Updike. *Rabbit, Run* tells the story of Harry "Rabbit" Angstrom, a former high school basketball star, now living with his pregnant, alcoholic wife and their young son. Rabbit can't stand it. As he says early on, when you are successful, it is hard to be third-rate, and that is what his life has become. He is demonstrating the Magi-Peeler at a local department store. Can you sink any lower than that? He comes home from work, shoots a little hoop with some neighborhood kids who suddenly realize how good he is, and suddenly he remembers how good he was. Once home, he finds his wife, Janice, drunk and glassy-eyed, watching *The Mickey Mouse Club*. In short order, Rabbit vanishes. First, he tries to escape by driving to Florida, but this is before GPS, so he gets lost in the tangle of pre-interstate highways in his home state of Pennsylvania. So he goes to see his old high school basketball coach for advice.

You might think that Coach would tell him to go back to his wife. Instead, Coach says that he has got a date in a little while with a woman, and he could have the woman bring a friend. Can you imagine how shocking this must have been to an early 1960s audience? Rabbit says, "Why not?" He goes on the date. The woman he dates is a semi-prostitute. Rabbit sleeps with her … and moves in.

Plot point one.

Act two covers the complications that ensue from Rabbit's decision to leave his wife and move in with another woman in the town not far from where he lives. We see the relationship between Rabbit and the other woman. We see the local minister play golf with Rabbit and try to talk sense into him. That doesn't end well. And we see Janice struggling through her pregnancy. And then she is about to give birth, so Rabbit comes home.

Plot point two.

Remember that we need three critical scenes in act three—the Big

Gloom, where everything appears lost; the Mano a Mano, where the two main characters have the conflict-ridden scene that they couldn't possibly have had unless everything in the story to this point has taken place; and then, the amazing ending. Buckle up. It is going to be a bumpy ride.

Rabbit comes home at the beginning of act three, and seemingly all is well. He is thrilled with the new baby, Janice is thrilled that he is back, and everything is terrific … until he asks for an unspecified action during sex that he obviously learned from the other woman. What was it? Updike didn't say. The imagination embroiders. And Janice is furious. She basically tells him, "If that is what you want, go back to your whore!"

Janice responds to the situation by getting drunk. She gives the baby a bath … and it drowns.

How is that for a Big Gloom?

So now, Janice and Rabbit finally have it out. This is the Mano a Mano, the conversation they couldn't have had if all those prior events had not taken place. And now, we need an amazing ending. A death requires a funeral. The funeral is in the woods. Rabbit can't take it, so he starts literally to run away from the burial, chased through the woods by the entire group of mourners. Under pressure, Janice gets drunk; Rabbit, by contrast, runs away from situations. And that is how the novel ends, with the entire funeral party running after Rabbit through the woods. The last sentence is "Rabbit runs. Ah: runs."

Wow.

If three act structure along the lines I have described here works well enough for *The Wizard of Oz* and *Rabbit, Run,* give it a try. It might just work for you.

I know I've thrown a ton at you. If we were at UCLA, I would have a full day to get all this material across. So if you want to go out and get a cigarette or make a couple of phone calls or check your feed, I will wait.

Oh, you are back! Great!

The third and final aspect of structure that I'd like to share with you is scene structure. Scenes are the building blocks of fiction, both novels and short stories. Here's the definition of scenes that we will use: "A scene is a situation involving conflict that begins and ends with a change in time and/or place." That is so important that I will repeat it:

"A scene is a situation involving conflict that begins and ends with a change in time and/or place." There must be conflict in every scene; a scene without conflict is an invitation to the reader to close the book. We say that either the time or the place has changed since the previous scene. That way, we know a new scene has begun. In fact, over the course of a novel, every scene is like a little three-act movie, typically no more than two or three pages in length, with only a few longer exceptions. Let's take a look at the three phases of a scene, so you understand what I'm talking about.

The first phase is what I call the setup. The setup can last only two paragraphs and must—yes, I said must—include three facts. They are: where are we, who is present, and how much time has passed since the previous scene. You can do it as simply as, "An hour later, Sam and Samantha entered the restaurant." Where are they? The restaurant. Who is there? Sam and Samantha. How much time has passed since the previous scene? An hour. You now have almost two full paragraphs to add in any kind of color or details as you see fit, but you must provide these three facts, because they ground a reader and tie what is about to happen to what has come before. Sometimes, I will ask the class whether anyone is carrying a novel with them. Back in the day, there would always be a few. I will have the person give me the book and I will it open it at the beginning of any random chapter. I will then read the first two paragraphs. Inevitably, those three points are answered. The class sees this as something of a magic trick. Again, great writers intuit this, while the rest of us, me included, need to be shown this fact.

The second phase of the scene, the longest phase, is conflict. Sam and Samantha are going to argue over something. If they just have a nice conversation, it is boring and it is not a scene and who cares? Instead, Sam wants to borrow $5,000 from Samantha. Samantha wants Sam to divorce his wife. I don't care what it is. They just have to be at odds over something. That is the conflict section.[1]

The third aspect of a scene is really just two sentences: the resolution and hook. We just had a conflict, and every conflict needs a resolution. Fortunately, there are only three possible resolutions to practically any conflict between two human beings—yes, no, and maybe later. Will Samantha loan Sam the money? Yes, no, or she tells him she will get back to him. Will Sam divorce his wife? Yes, he agrees; no, he refuses; or he tells Samantha he will think it over and get back to her. That is the resolution. It is that simple.

Next comes the hook. A hook is a one sentence device that drives the reader forward into the next scene. "He turned and left the restaurant." Where did he go? "She took out her phone and began to text." Who is she texting? "The doorbell rang, and he went to see who was there." Unanswered questions keep readers moving forward. If there is no hook, again, it is an invitation to close the book.

Once again, I will pick up the novel that the student gave me and turn to the ending of a chapter, because for most authors, the end of a chapter is the end of a scene. Sure enough, just like magic, we will find a resolution and hook taking up no more than two sentences. It looks like magic, but it is just solid scene structure. I will then demonstrate that a novel is simply a collection of scenes, and scenes are simply a conga line of setup, conflict, resolution, hook, setup, conflict, resolution, hook. I will actually stand up there and, in a silly fashion, demonstrate a conga line with the words "setup, conflict, resolution, hook." And then I will tell the students, "Now, you are no longer 'writing a novel,' which sounds like a lot of work. Instead, you

---

1 To truly understand the nature of conflict in scenes, may I recommend Lajos Egri's seminal work, *The Art of Dramatic Writing*. And thank you, Lew Hunter, for turning me to Lajos Egri back in 1988.

are simply writing the conflict section of scene six in act two, and you know that you are probably about six or eight scenes until you get to the next plot point."

Okay, I don't know about you, but I'm exhausted. I just telescoped eight hours of teaching into one chapter. The good news is that now you know everything I know about story construction, three act construction, and scene construction. Use it, trust it, go forth, and sin no more.

ABOUT THE AUTHOR

Michael Levin has been called the "Michael Jordan of private biography." Over a 30-year career, Michael has written, co-written, edited, ghosted, or published **more than a thousand books. Two are** *New York Times* **best sellers, more than two dozen are legitimate national best sellers**, and **three are Amazon number one bestselling business books**.

His websites are www.MichaelLevinWrites.com and, for business fiction/business fables, www.TheFableFactory.com.

Michael appeared on the first episode of Season Three of **ABC's Shark Tank**, has appeared on **BBC worldwide TV and radio** and **Good Morning, America**, and has been quoted in **Inc. Magazine**, and in **BloombergBusiness**. He is most proud of having edited **Zig Ziglar**'s final book, *Born to Win*.

He is also one of the most frequently published commentators on culture and the arts in the United States, with more than 400 pieces published on outlets including **the New York Times, The Wall Street Journal, Forbes, Politico.com, FoxNews.com, HuffPost, Forbes. com, the Boston Globe, the Los Angeles Times, Robb Report, Worth.com, Writers Digest, ESPN, and the New York Daily News.** Many of his pieces have attracted more than one million readers.

His books have received **outstanding reviews** in **The New York Times, The New Yorker, People Magazine, The New York Times**

(daily and Sunday), Los Angeles Times, Fortune/CNN Money, Washington Post, The Boston Globe, Esquire, Newsweek, San Francisco Examiner, and **Publishers Weekly.**

Michael has co-written with **Baseball Hall of Famer Dave Winfield**, *Dropping The Ball* (Scribner 2007), Los Angeles Times best seller); **football broadcasting legend Pat Summerall**, *Giants—What I Learned About Life From Vince Lombardi and Tom Landry* (Wiley 2010); **Hollywood publicist Howard Bragman**, *Where's My Fifteen Minutes?* (Penguin/Portfolio 2008), national best seller); **FBI undercover agent Joaquin Garcia** *Making Jack Falcone* **(Simon & Schuster/Touchstone 2008), New York Times best seller, featured on 60 Minutes and optioned by Steven Soderbergh and Paramount**; former Schwab CEO David Pottruck, *Stacking the Deck* (Jossey-Bass 2011), New York Times best seller); **Rock and Roll Fantasy Camp founder David Fishof**, *Rock Your Business!* (Ben Bella 2012), **#1 Amazon Kindle Business best seller**); and **E-Myth creator Michael Gerber**; three-time **Super Bowl winner Chad Hennings** of the Dallas Cowboys; **Fox Sports broadcaster Chris Myers**; NBA star Doug Christie; **marketing legend Jay Abraham**; and **NFL star running backs Maurice Jones-Drew and Benjamin Watson**.

He has written more than 100 books for wealth managers, family offices, financial advisors, and top insurance professionals, including individuals at Morgan Stanley, UBS, Wells Fargo, LPL Financial, Atria Wealth Solutions, and many other leading institutions.

Michael is married and has four children. In the past 20 years, Michael has completed more than 40 long-distance races—20 marathons, including 11 Boston Marathons, for which he has raised more than $200,000 for the Dana-Farber Cancer Institute. He has served in 10 marathons as a guide runner for runners with disabilities for Achilles International. Michael won his black belt in tae kwan do at age 54, alongside his twin sons. In 2021, Michael became a Certified Yoga Instructor. A trained tenor, he performed for years with the Tanglewood Festival Chorus in Boston's Symphony Hall, Carnegie Hall, and Tanglewood. He has sung Beethoven's 9th Symphony with choruses on three continents – in Boston, London, and Jerusalem.

SELECTED COWRITTEN AND GHOSTWRITTEN BOOKS NONFICTION

Coauthor, *Rock Your Business! Turning Your Idea into Reality … Satisfaction … and a Whole Lot of Cold, Hard Cash*, by **David Fishof**, founder of the Rock 'N Roll Fantasy Camp. (BenBella Books 2012) **National best seller and number one Amazon Kindle business best seller**

Cowriter, *Dropping the Ball*, by Hall-of-Fame baseball player **Dave Winfield** (Scribner 2007). **Reached #2 on the Los Angeles Times nonfiction best seller list. The New York Times called it "unusually thoughtful;" the Boston Globe called it "eloquent," and it was deemed "recommended reading" in Esquire Magazine. National bestseller.**

Coauthor, *Where's My Fifteen Minutes? How To Win Friends and Influence People in the Media Age* by **Howard Bragman** (Penguin/Portfolio 2009)

Reached #10 on the national Barnes&Nobel.com best sellers list.

Ghostwriter, *The Sticking Point* by **Jay Abraham** (Vanguard Books 2009)

Reached #2 on multiple Amazon.com business best seller lists.

Ghostwriter, *The Real Rules of Life* by **Ken Druck** (Hay House 2012)

Ghostwriter, *How To Be An All-Pro Father (Even If It's Your First Time Being A Dad),* by NFL star **Benjamin Watson** (Baker Books 2016)

NATIONAL BESTSELLER

Coauthor, *NASCAR Nation, How Racing's Values Mirror the Nation's* by Fox Sports Reporter **Chris Myers** (Random House 2012)

MEMOIRS

Coauthor, *Making Jack Falcone* by **Joaquin Garcia**, the true story of the FBI agent who infiltrated the Mafia and took down the top 32 members of the Gambino crime family, (Simon and Schuster/Touchstone 2008)

New York Times bestseller. Optioned by Paramount for Steven Soderbergh, director of Traffic, Erin Brockovich, and Ocean's 11. Featured on 60 Minutes.

Coauthor, *Lift Your Voice—How The Killing Of My Nephew George Floyd Changed The World* by **Angela Harrelson** (George Floyd's aunt) (Post Hill Press 2022)

Featured in People Magazine; audio deal with Audible

Coauthor, *Giants—What I Learned About Life from Vince Lombardi and Tom Landry* by NFL legend **Pat Summerall** (Wiley 2010)

Featured in Newsweek, ESPN, etc.

Coauthor, *Welcome Home, Boris and Mama,* by **Carey Neesley** (Readers Digest Books 2013)

Excerpted in Readers Digest Magazine

Coauthor, *Rules of Engagement*, with **Chad Hennings**, three-time Super Bowl winner with the Dallas Cowboys and a fighter pilot in the first Gulf War, who flew 45 humanitarian missions to the Kurds (FaithWorks 2010)

Coauthor, *No Ordinary Love*, by NBA star **Doug Christie** and his wife **Jackie Christie**

Coauthor, *Banking on our Future*, by Operation Hope founder Ambassador **John Bryant** (Beacon Press 2002)

BUSINESS FABLES AND FICTION

Coauthor, *When All Else Fails, Sell!* by **David Oliphant** (Readers Digest Books 2012)

Ghostwritten novel (2009)—governed by nondisclosure agreement **Optioned by both HBO and ABC and became a hit TV series on ABC**

Coauthor, *Lunch Money Can't Shoot,* a young adult novel with **Jack Pannell**, (Morgan James 2017) **Amazon Bestseller**

ACKNOWLEDGMENTS

First and foremost, I'd like to thank Mary Fearon, who had the idea for this book. Mary and the branding company she runs, OnPrpose, looked at the ghostwriting industry in general and spoke with past clients of ours. Mary concluded that our company is better than anyone at identifying what's most meaningful in the careers, personal lives, and outside interests of individuals. She suggested that we focus on meaning as the raison d'etre for our company. And that's what we've done. So Mary, thank you for your brilliant ideas, and I hope this book matches up with what you intended me to write.

Thanks to all who read and commented on various drafts – Todd Chobotar, Cynthia Granger, Rena Vegh, Bracha Fliegelman, and Justin Batt.

Thank you to my awesome publishing partner, Patricia Bacall Garver, and her brilliant copy editor, Gillian MacDonald.

Kudos to my fantastic photographer and video guy, David Beyda, who did the cover image as well as the welcome videos on our website.

Thank you, Michael Knudsen, my web designer and webmaster for more than two decades. Your creativity and dedication have been foundational for me for such a long time.

And finally, my thanks as always to my wife Suzanne for her love and support.

www.ingramcontent.com/pod-product-compliance
Lightning Source LLC
Chambersburg PA
CBHW040734120726
48010CB00016B/379/J